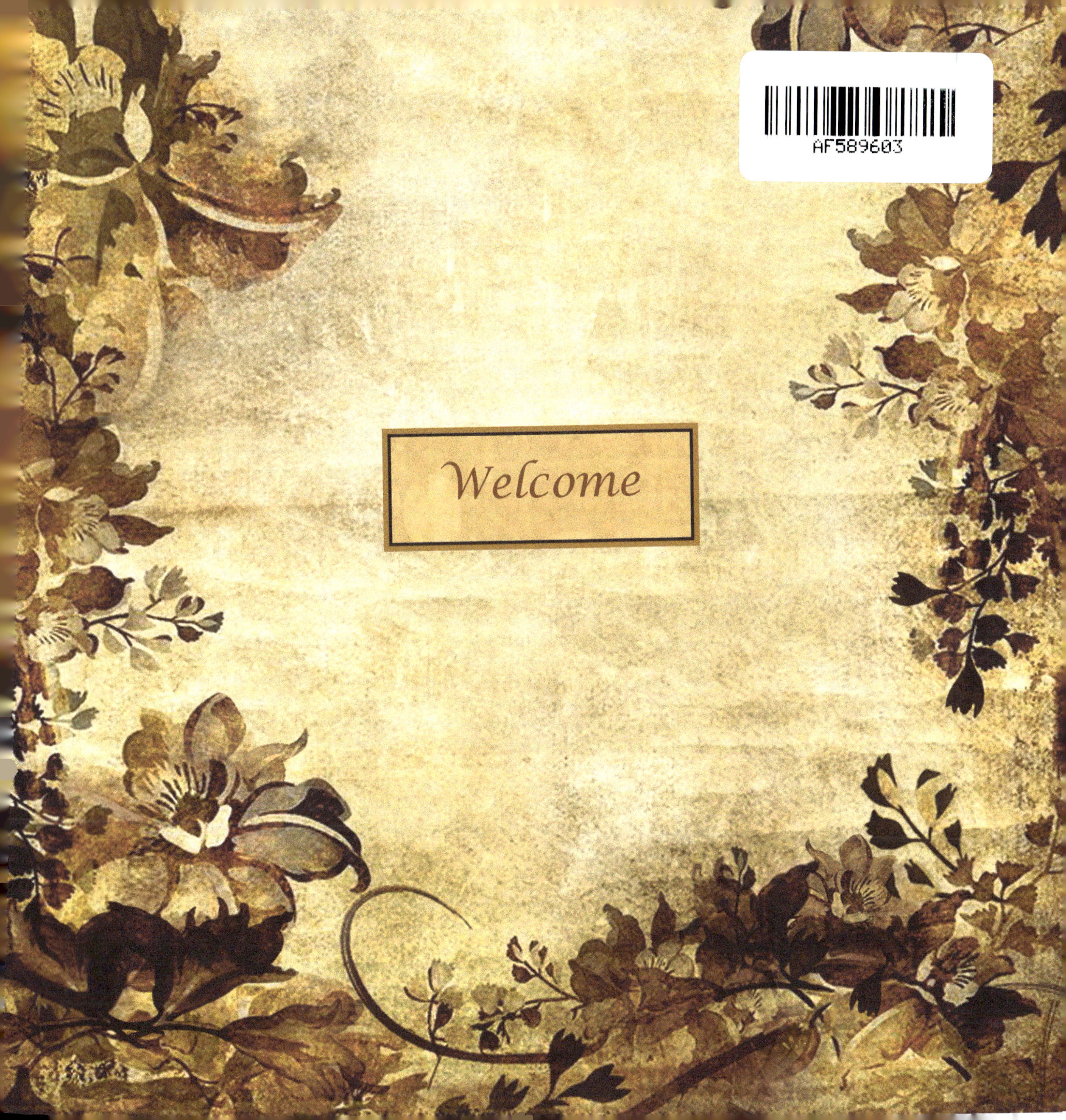
Welcome

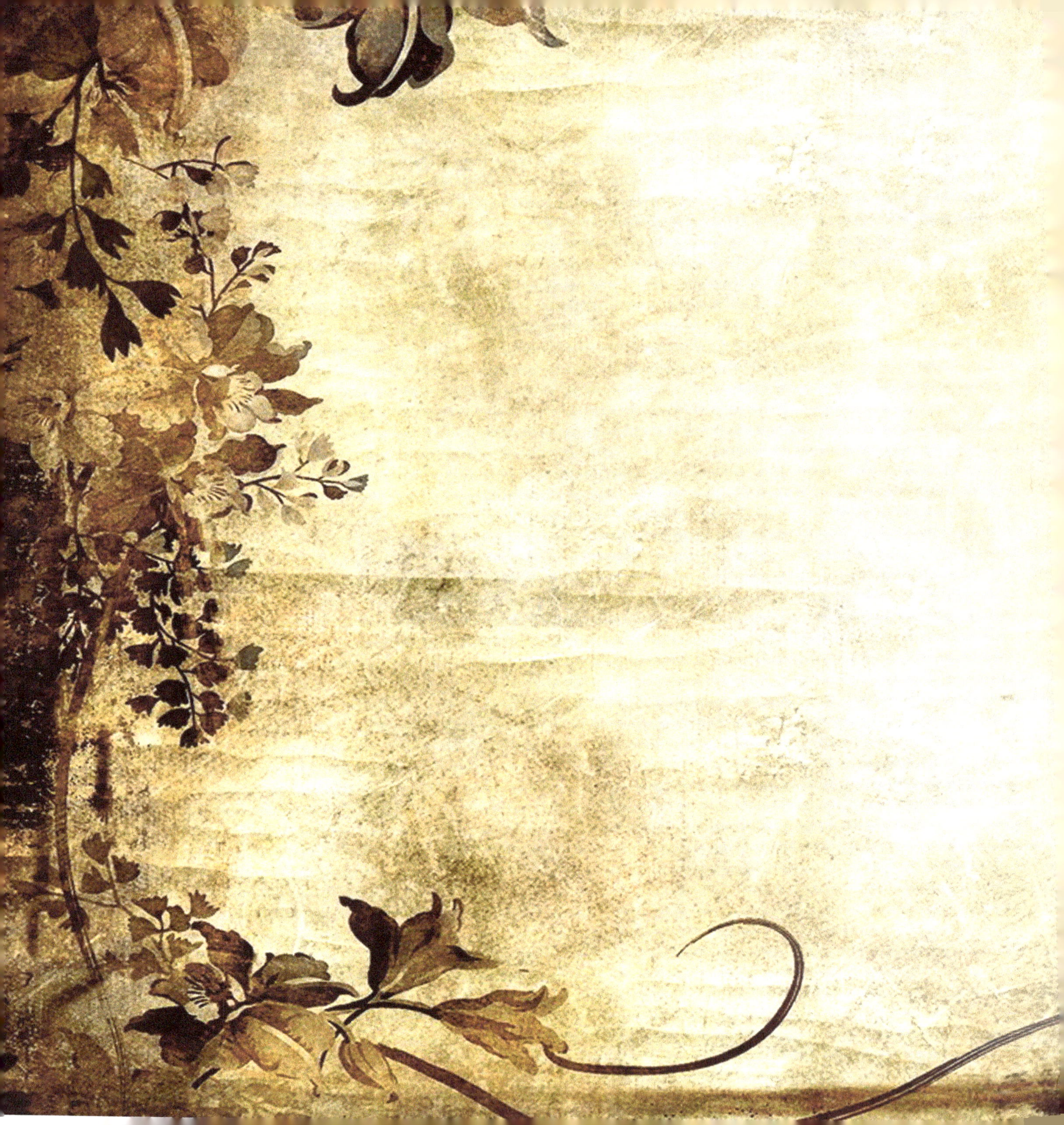

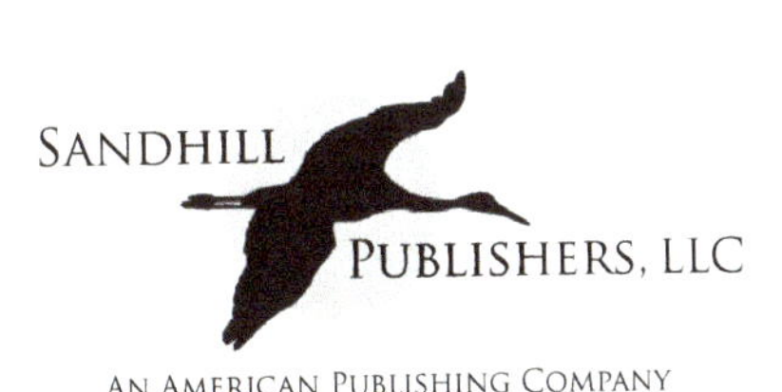
SANDHILL
PUBLISHERS, LLC
AN AMERICAN PUBLISHING COMPANY

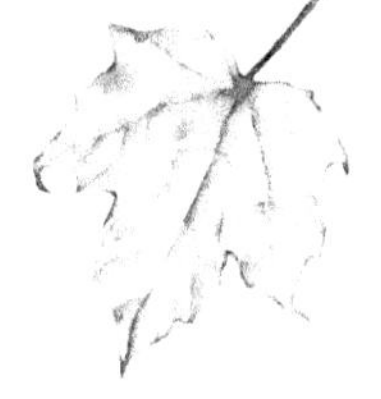

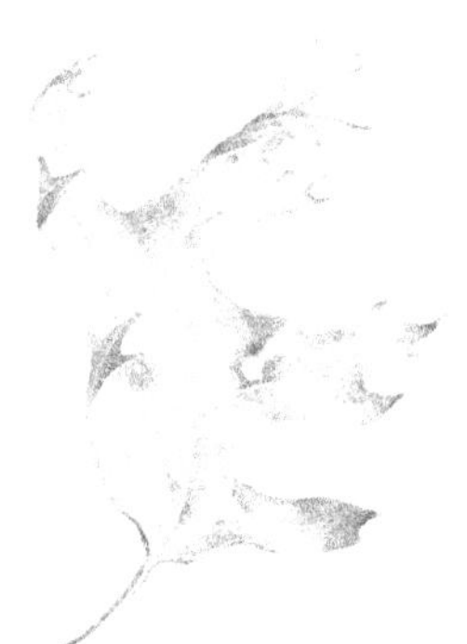

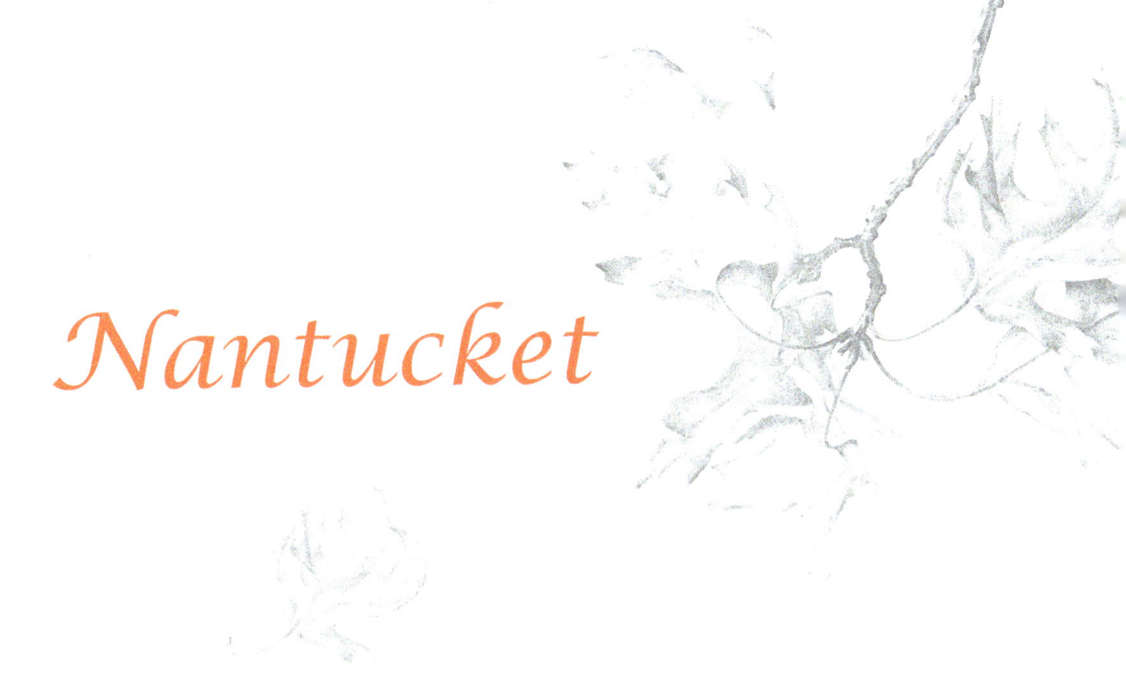

Nantucket

Daffodil Festival

Book Two

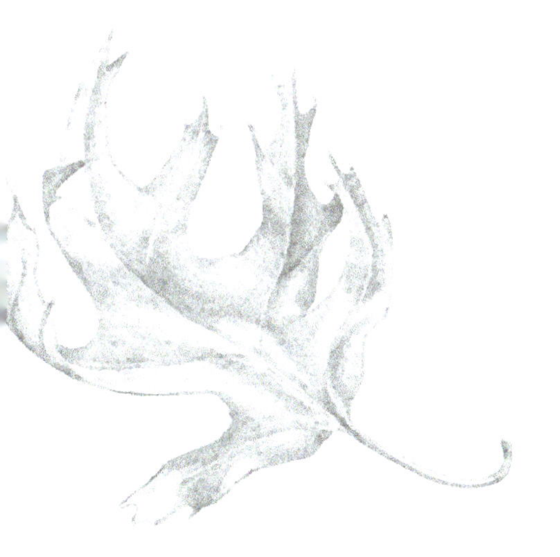

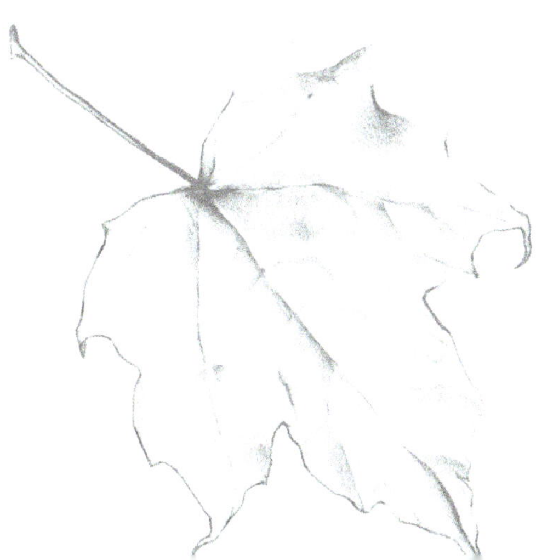

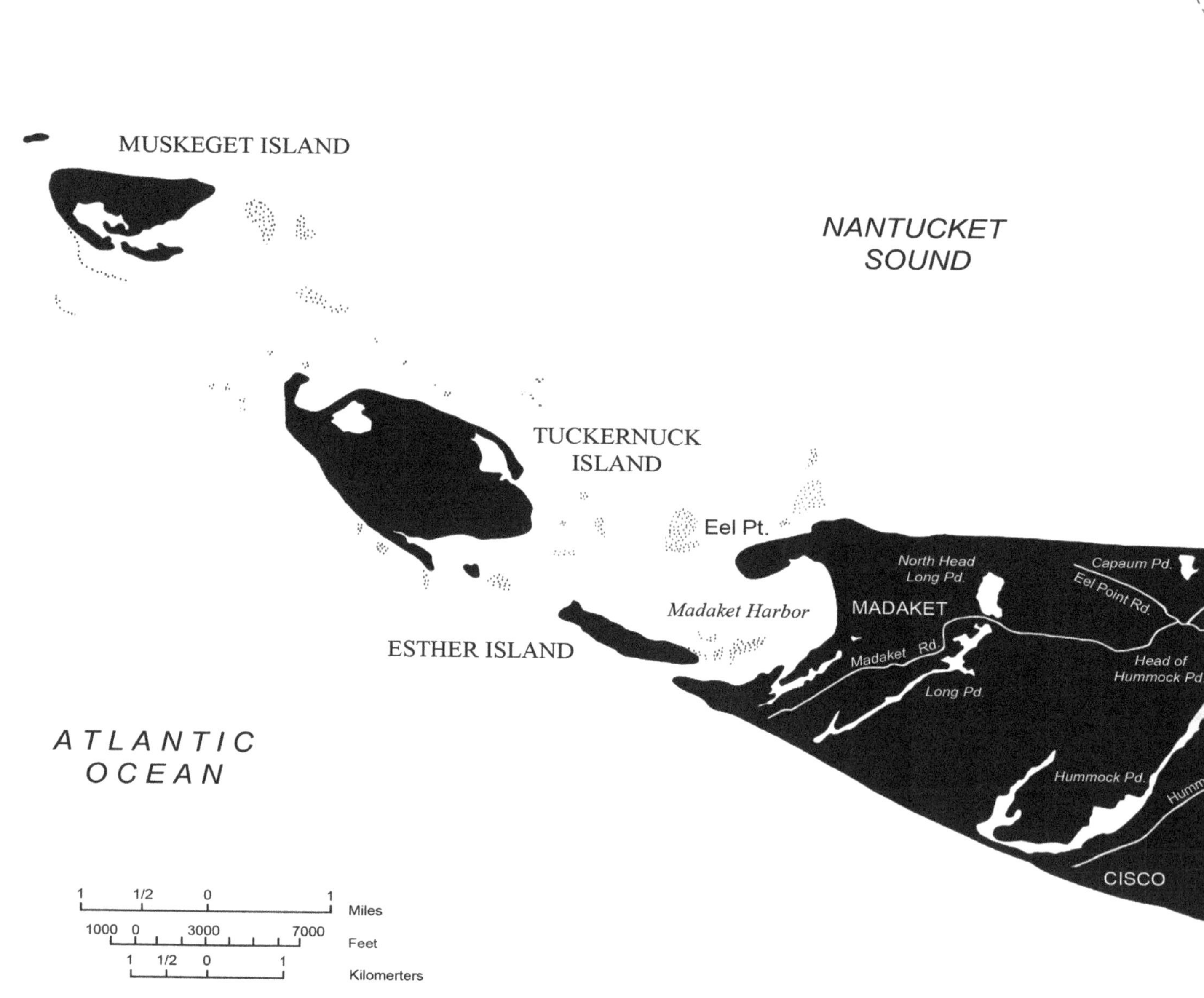
FERRY ROUTE
MUSKEGET ISLAND
NANTUCKET SOUND
TUCKERNUCK ISLAND
Eel Pt.
North Head Long Pd.
Capaum Pd.
Eel Point Rd.
MADAKET
Madaket Harbor
ESTHER ISLAND
Madaket Rd.
Head of Hummock Pd.
Long Pd.
ATLANTIC OCEAN
Hummock Pd.
CISCO
1 1/2 0 1
Miles
1000 0 3000 7000
Feet
1 1/2 0 1
Kilomerters

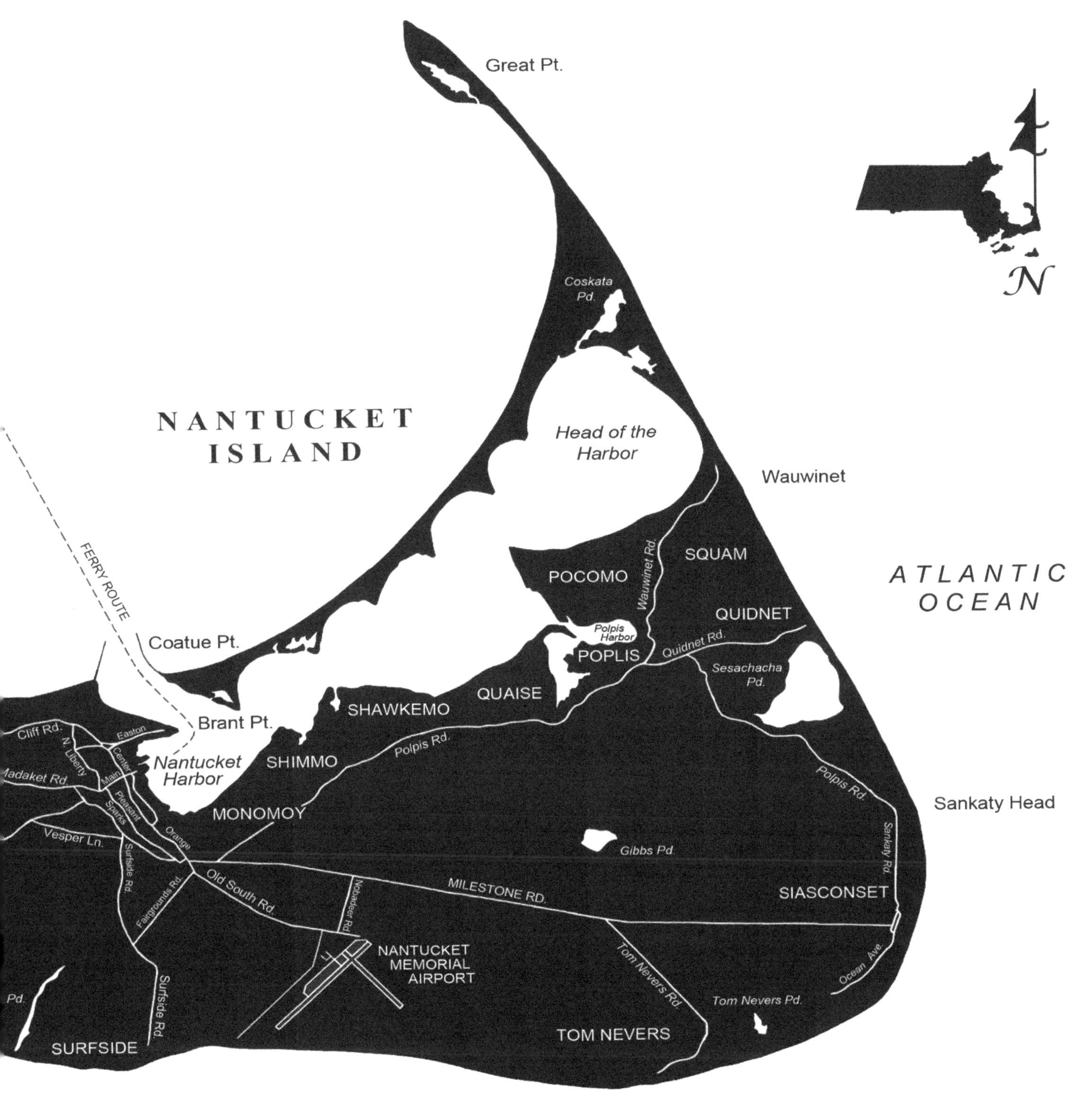
NANTUCKET
ISLAND
Great Pt.
Coskata Pd.
Head of the Harbor
Wauwinet
ATLANTIC
OCEAN
N
FERRY ROUTE
Coatue Pt.
Brant Pt.
Nantucket Harbor
POCOMO
SQUAM
QUIDNET
Wauwinet Rd.
Polpis Harbor
POPLIS
Quidnet Rd.
Sesachacha Pd.
QUAISE
SHAWKEMO
SHIMMO
MONOMOY
Polpis Rd.
Cliff Rd.
Easton
N. Liberty
Center
Madaket Rd.
Main
Pleasant
Sparks
Orange
Vesper Ln.
Surfside Rd.
Fairgrounds Rd.
Old South Rd.
Nobadeer Rd.
MILESTONE RD.
Gibbs Pd.
Sankaty Head
Sankaty Rd.
SIASCONSET
Ocean Ave.
NANTUCKET
MEMORIAL
AIRPORT
Tom Nevers Rd.
Tom Nevers Pd.
TOM NEVERS
Pd.
Surfside Rd.
SURFSIDE

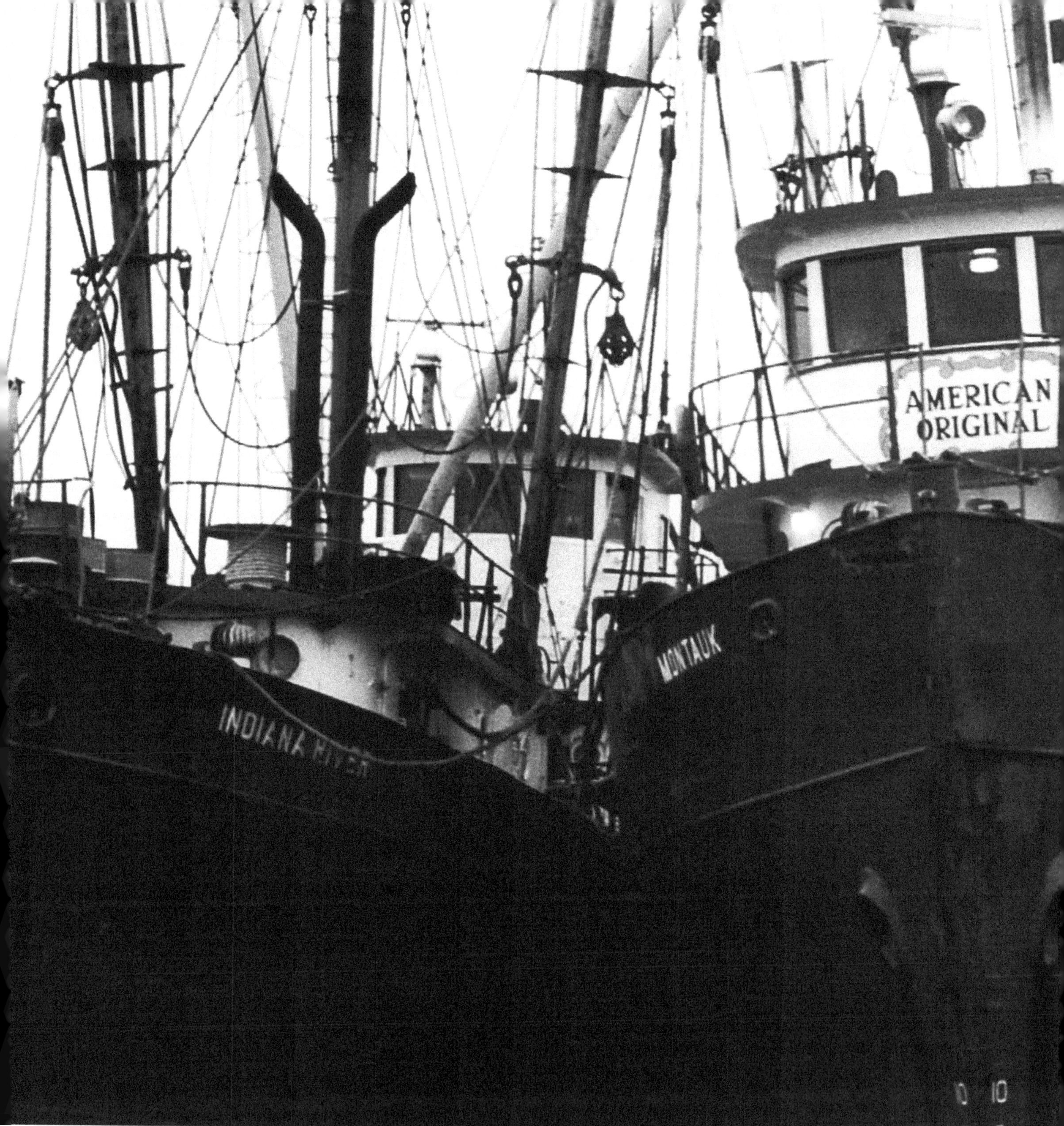
AMERICAN
ORIGINAL
MONTAUK
INDIANA

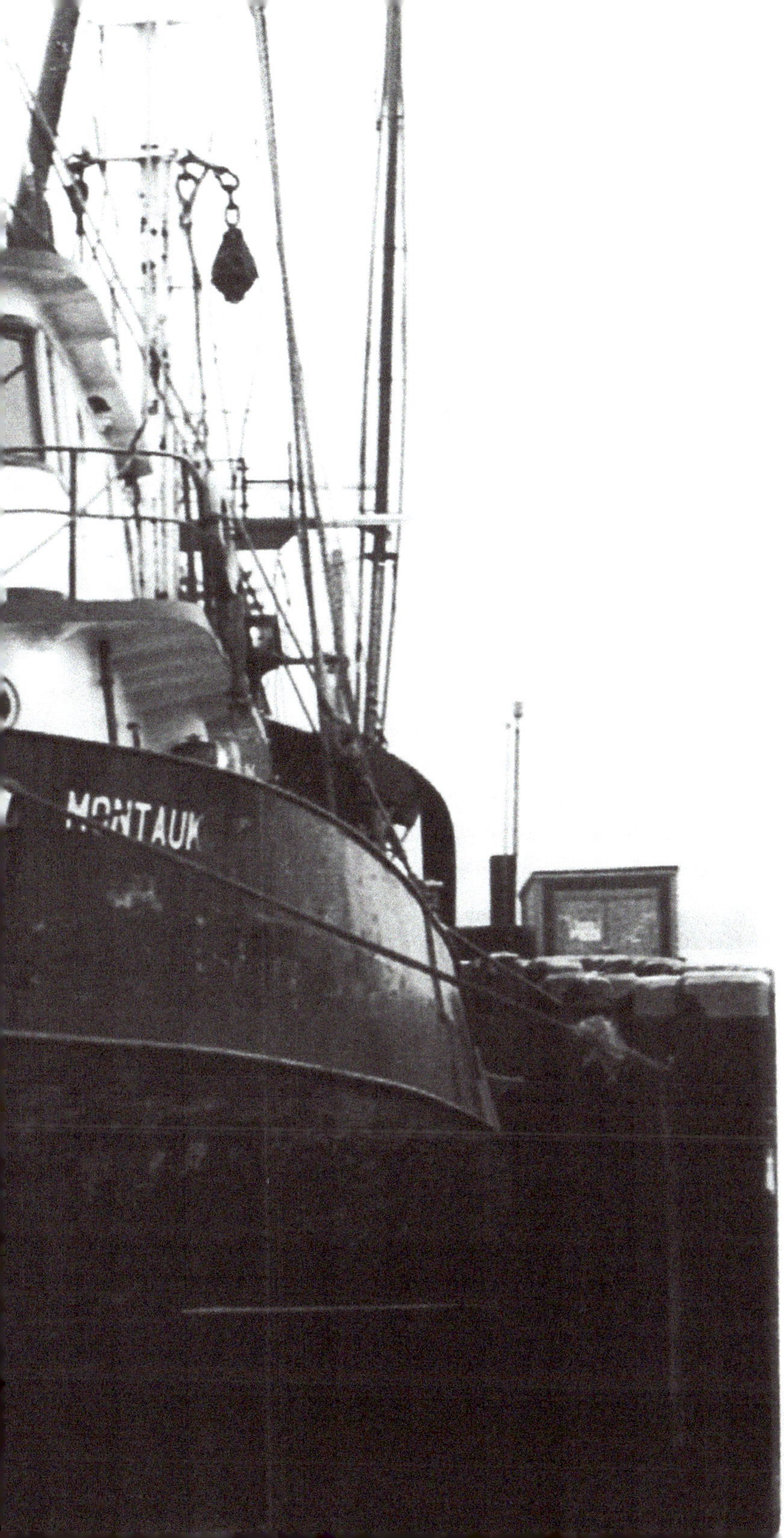

For Willa S. and Ann S.

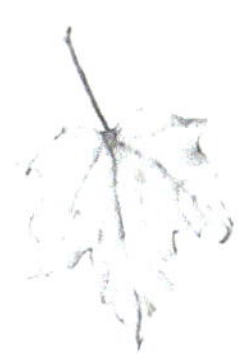

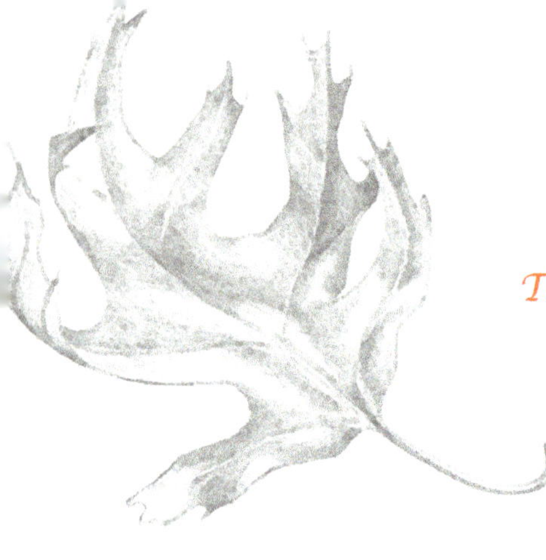

This pictorial essay was inspired by true events

First Edition - Softcover
Book Design by T. C. Bartlett
Editors: Willa Stiber, Panda S., Kim Gantt

For publishing & licensing rights contact: T. C. Bartlett at: tc@tcbartlett.com
Sandhill Publishers, LLC, Nashville, Indiana
Publisher/Registered Agent: Andrew B. Simms contact: sandhillpublishers.com

Printed in the United States of America
Library of Congress Control Number: 2018934161

ISBN-13 978-0-9984716-3-1
ISBN-10 0-998-4716-3-1

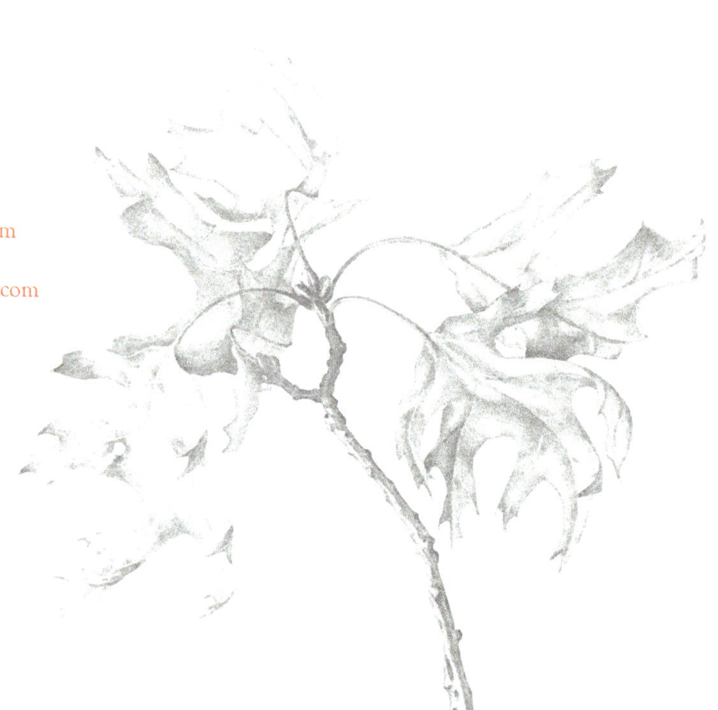

Nantucket

Daffodil Festival

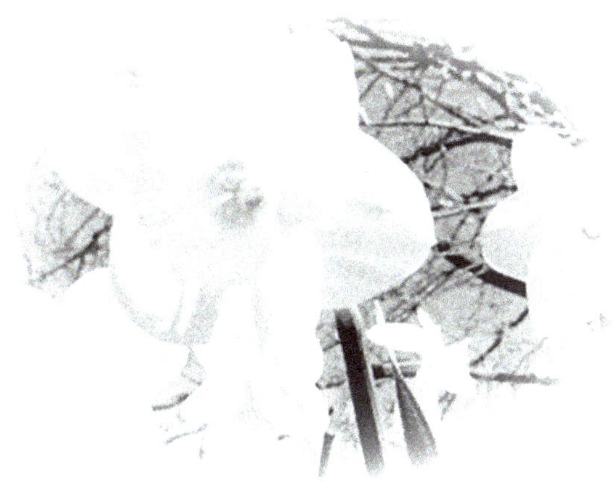

From the journal: This Is My Nantucket

by

Jack Blade

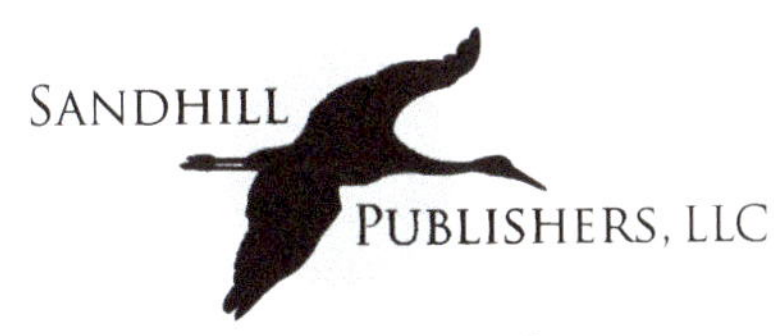

INTRODUCTION BY ANN LOUISE

Meeting Jack

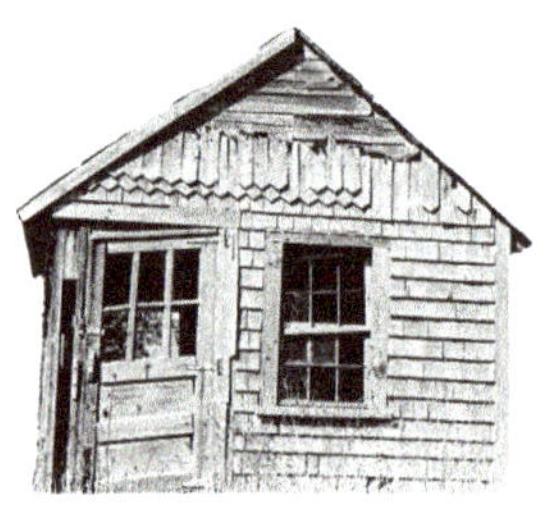

For those of you who haven't read Jack Blade's first Nantucket book, *Nantucket Island Images*, I've included the introduction which explains about Jack and the photographs he took while he lived and worked on Nantucket during the years between 1979 and 1982.

And for those of you who already know the Jack story, I proudly give you his second Nantucket photo essay, *Nantucket Daffodil Festival.* — *Ann Louise*

There is a charming, unassuming house on the outskirts of a small town in Southern Indiana. It is a clapboard saltbox-style and shutterless structure, standing prim and proper and starched as a Quaker garment, in dove gray paint and cream-colored trim. One could easily imagine an author scribbling away in this house, pencil to paper.

The past owner was a man named Jack Blade, and the home he had lived in reminded us of a particular street, Foster Street, in Cambridge, Massachusetts, which is celebrated for its uniquely small houses, known as the Cambridge dollhouses. My husband and I fell in love with it at first sight and have quickly made it our own.

To add to its charm, the house sits on about ten acres, with a large wooded frontage of maple, oak, redbud, and dogwood. In the back it boasts views of a mature hardwood forest, where four finger ridges jut out into a ravine. When it rains, the runoff water washes down along well-worn shelves of rock and spills into the creek one hundred feet below.

It's hard for me to explain how restful and peaceful my husband and I felt when we entered this house for the first time, never expecting to find such a treasure within.

My husband and I purchased the house in the summer of 2013 at Jack's estate sale. During the sale, we purchased a few pieces of furniture and several oriental rugs that suited the house perfectly.

One piece of furniture was an antique kneehole desk. The desk has six side drawers: three on one side of the kneehole, and three on the other. A slender three-inch drawer was also neatly seated in the middle, above the kneehole. Each drawer was locked.

At the closing, the attorney for Jack's estate handed us one last document to sign. A transfer of ownership of all contents inside the antique desk. The attorney said to us: . . . *"I'm so pleased you purchased Jack's desk. Just so you know, Jack stipulated in his Will if no one purchased the desk during the estate sale, it was to be burned—and the ashes scattered with his own."* The attorney shook our hands, then handed us an envelope and the key to Jack's beguiling, but suspicious desk. All of which was quite intriguing and added a noteworthy mystery, and strength of character to Jack's house.

We knew exactly what we were going to do when we opened the front door and walked inside our

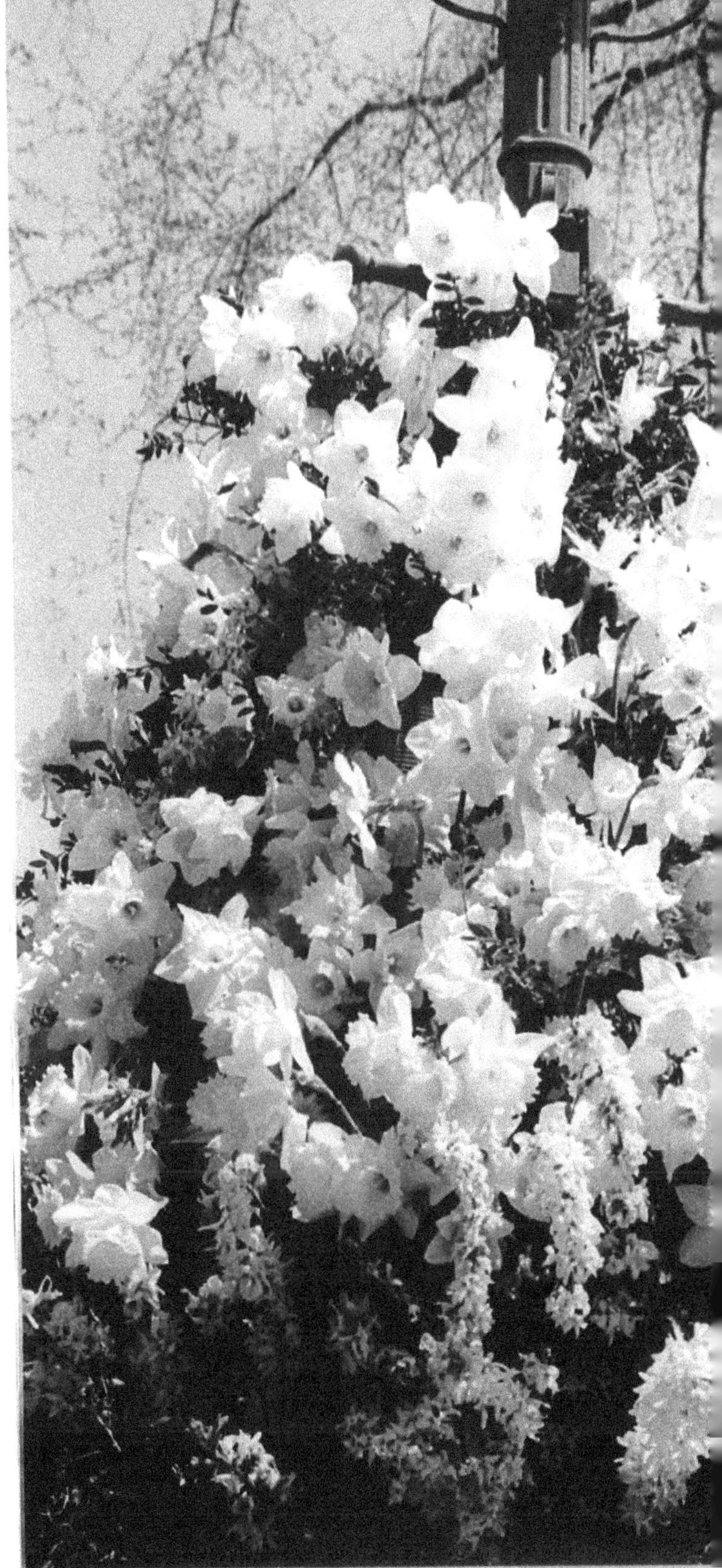

new home—find out what had been so purposely kept under lock and key in that mystifying desk.

We weren't disappointed.

We found the life's work of Jack Blade: the journals he'd kept, the stories he'd written, thousands of black-and-white photos he'd taken, the drawings he'd sketched, along with 35mm slides of abstract paintings he'd created, and the love letters he'd written to a certain Martha J. Kensington.

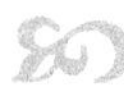

And that is how I met Jack.

For the past few years, I have been compiling all his manuscripts, photos, and love letters. I must admit, too, while I've been working on this manuscript, it has been somewhat frustrating not being able to get a real glimpse of the man Jack Blade. In a way, I've become haunted by that thought.

My research into the life of Jack Blade brought forth very little information. When I questioned Jack's neighbors, they said they never took the time to get to know him and that he was quiet, always keeping to himself. I did learn when Jack's parents became ill, he returned home, purchased this house, moved them in and became their home caregiver.

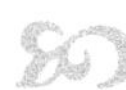

There are more than a hundred stories and love letters he had written to Martha J. Kensington.

His love letters to his Martha were in unsealed envelopes, neatly arranged in small bundles, and wrapped with a blue silk ribbon—all of which were stamped, but never mailed. Martha Kensington was

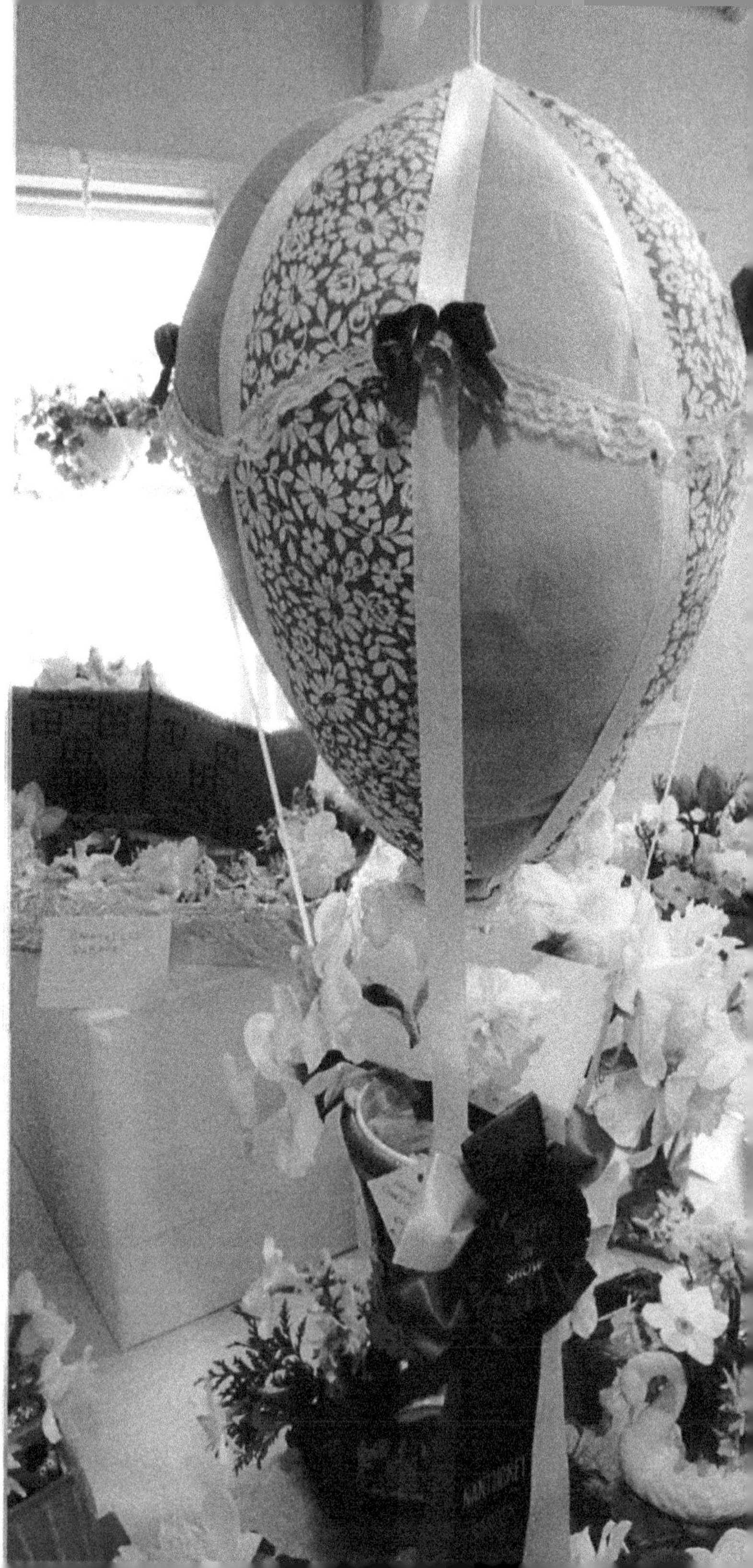

Jack's High School sweetheart who was killed in a car crash one year after graduating High School. Jack wrote:

— Saturday (my birthday), May 13, 1972
Made love under the stars with my one true love Martha, for the first time.
— Sunday, May 13, 1973
That was one year ago to this very day. I had no idea that it would be my only time. Need a place to find myself and figure out who I am and where I'm going. Without Martha, I am lost . . .

He was an old-school writer, never using a computer or even a typewriter. All of his writings are handwritten, pencil and pen on paper. It has taken quite an effort for us to assemble all his photos. It was something my husband and I knew we had to do. We never imagined we would ever be doing something like this. I believe it was meant to be that my husband and I were the ones to find all of Jack's journals and photographs.

In Jack's Nantucket journal, which he titled, *This is My Nantucket*, Jack writes:

Friday, June 29, 1979 — Nantucket Island

Arrived on Nantucket yesterday (renting a basement apartment on Plumb Lane just off of Main Street), and I am already looking for work so I can stay around this quaint whalers village for a while. I feel I have walked back in time. I need to get to know this place.

There is magic here . . .

Jack lived and worked on Nantucket from 1979 to 1982, and he took more than five thousand black and white photographs of the island. In his Nantucket Journal, he had sketched out the design for three books, *Island Images, Daffodil Festival,* and *Christmas Stroll.* I followed the layout of Jack's Nantucket books exactly as Jack had designed them, except for adding excerpts from his travel journals.

He took so many beautiful photos, it is was difficult to decide which ones should be used.

I wish you could see all of them.

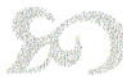

Having said all that, I give you Jack's photos and private thoughts from his journal, *This is My Nantucket*.

— *Ann Louise*

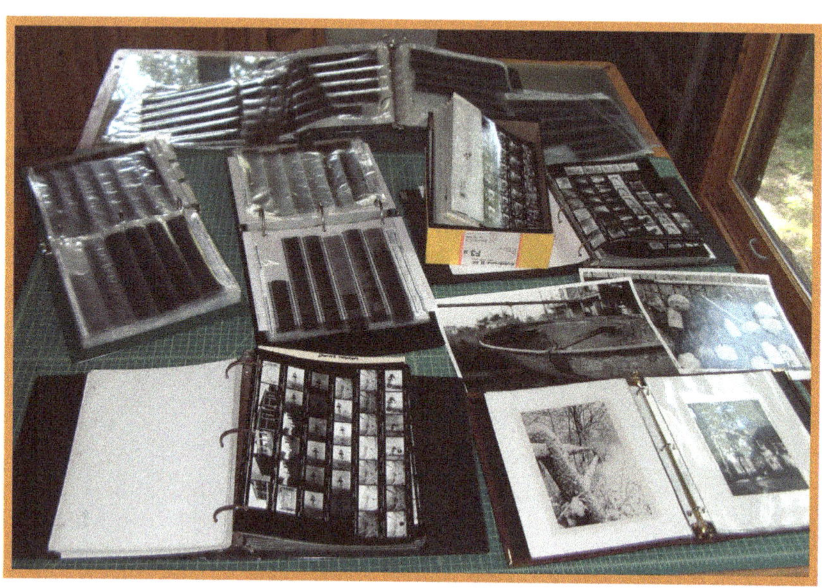

Jack's Negatives and Photos

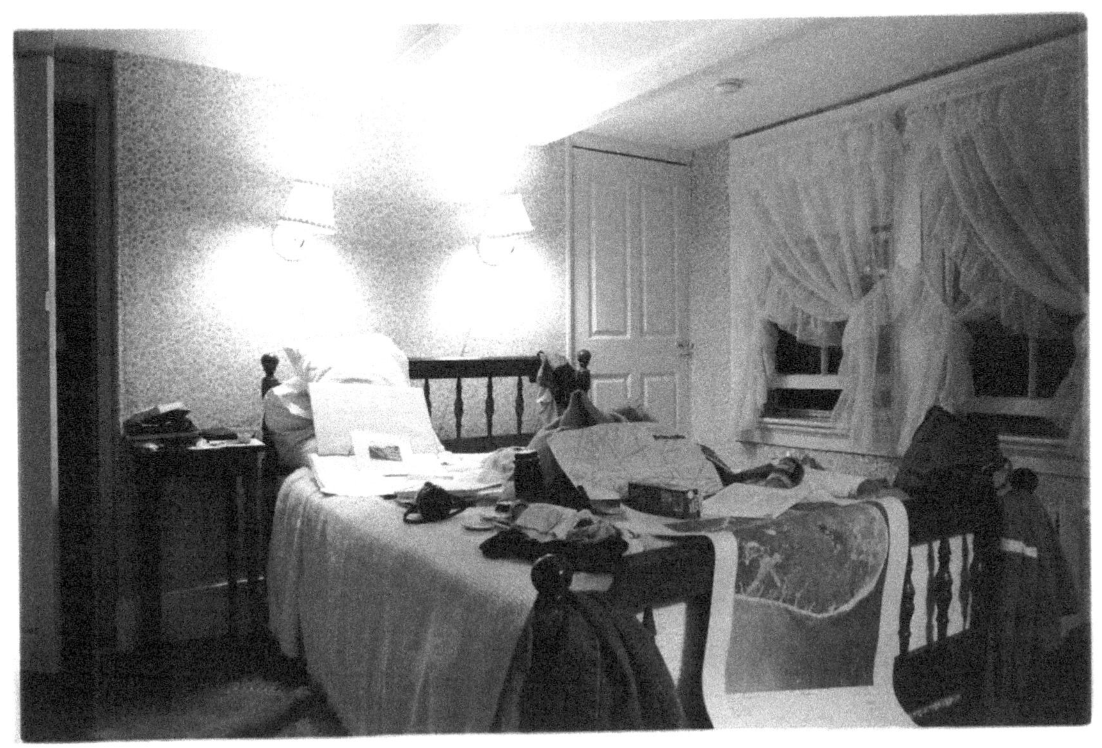

Jack's room when he first arrived on Nantucket in 1979

Nantucket Island
Saturday, April 1980

Spring can be measured by the advancement of its flowers, encouraged by some secret encrypted message to sprout.

This is my first spring on Nantucket, and I am pleasantly greeted with the beauty of the daffodil. They are the first to trumpet in random patches lining creek beds, front yards, gardens and along the roadside. You've never seen so many sprites dancing a jig all over the island.

This blossoming, and the advent of spring itself run rampant on Nantucket. Seeing this yellow petaled flower quickly washes away the frosty days and freezing nights of a Nantucket winter.

It is no great wonder why Nantucketers celebrate the spring and have a parade for the daffodil.

I applaud and say,
"Bravo!"

Excerpt from Jack's journal
This Is My Nantucket

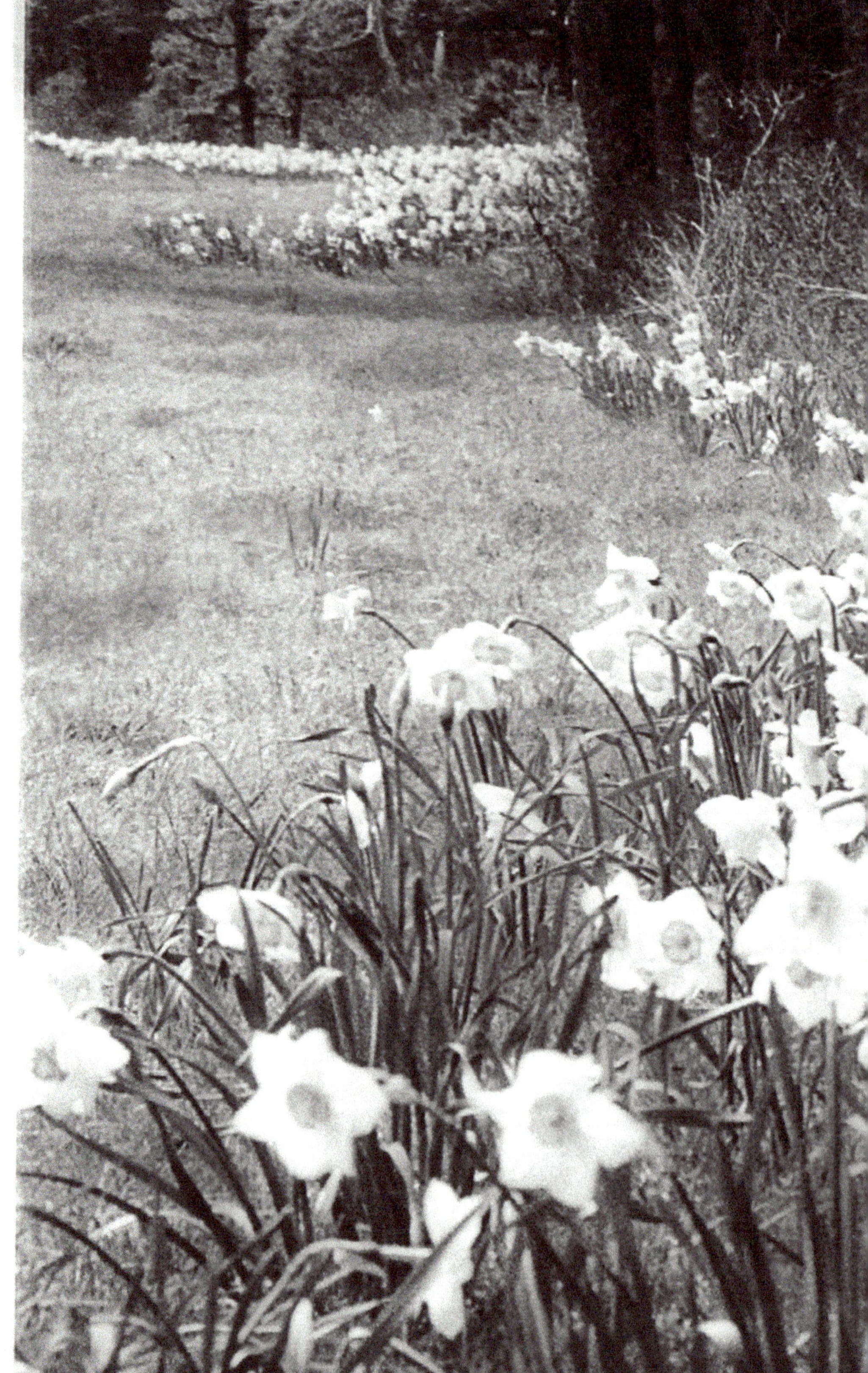

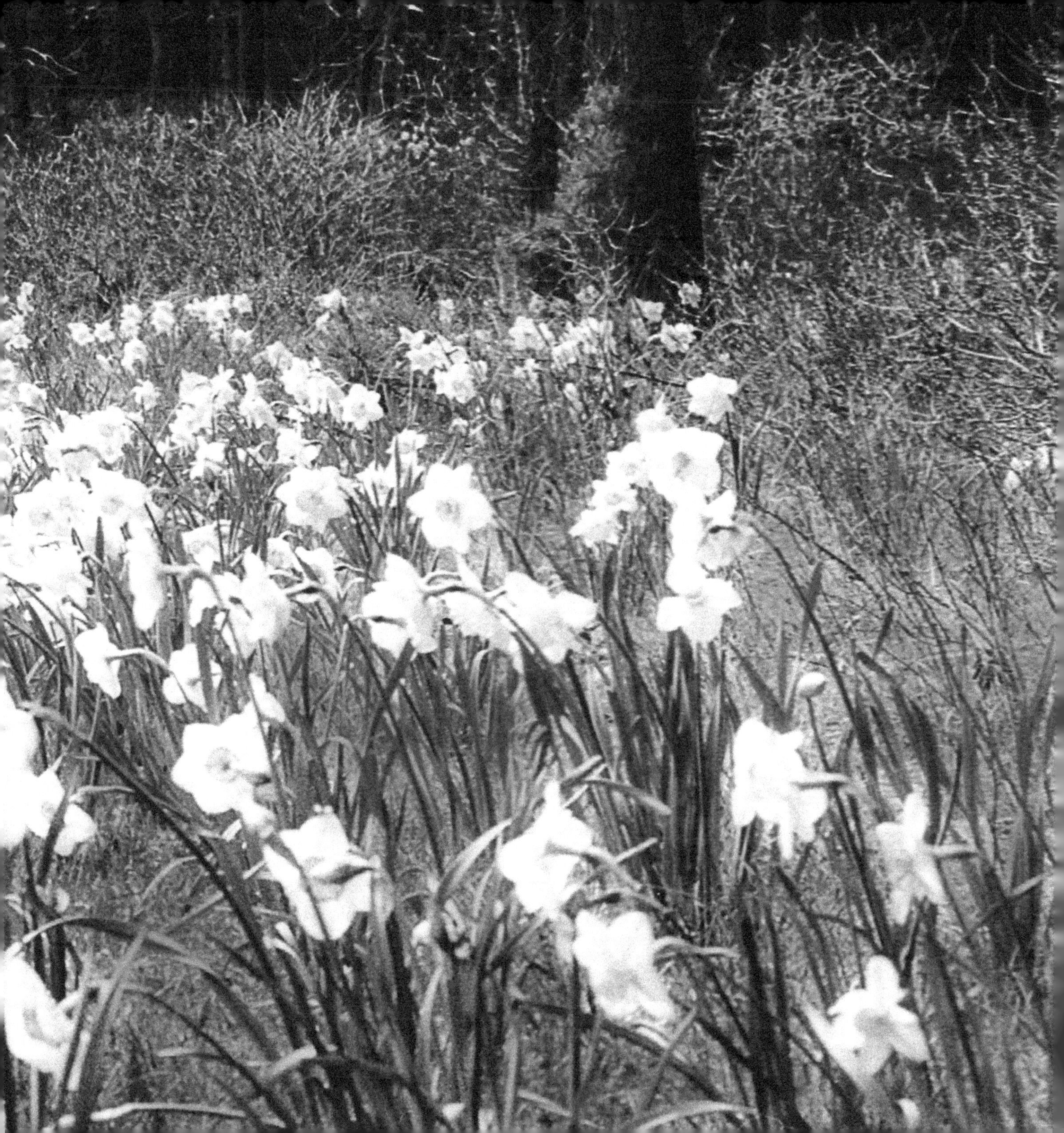

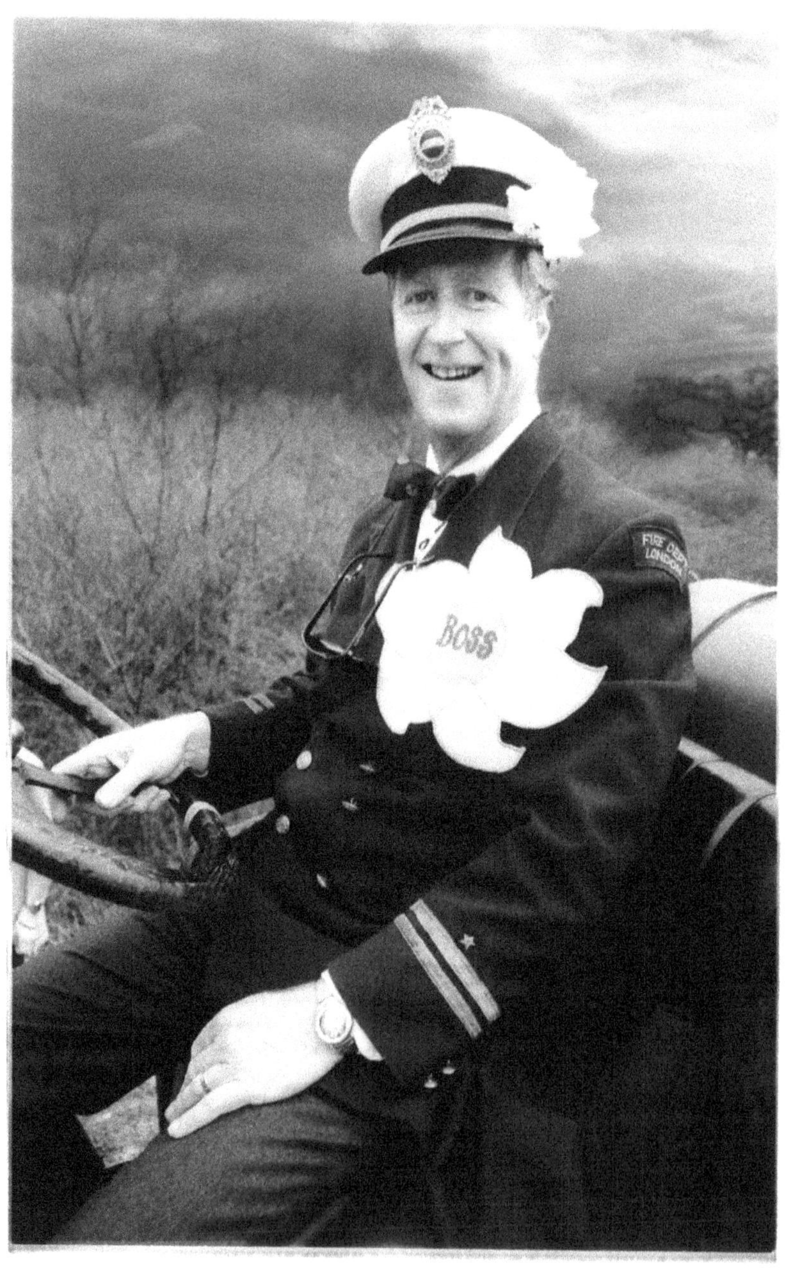

The Boss of The Parade - Wauwinet Fire Marshal

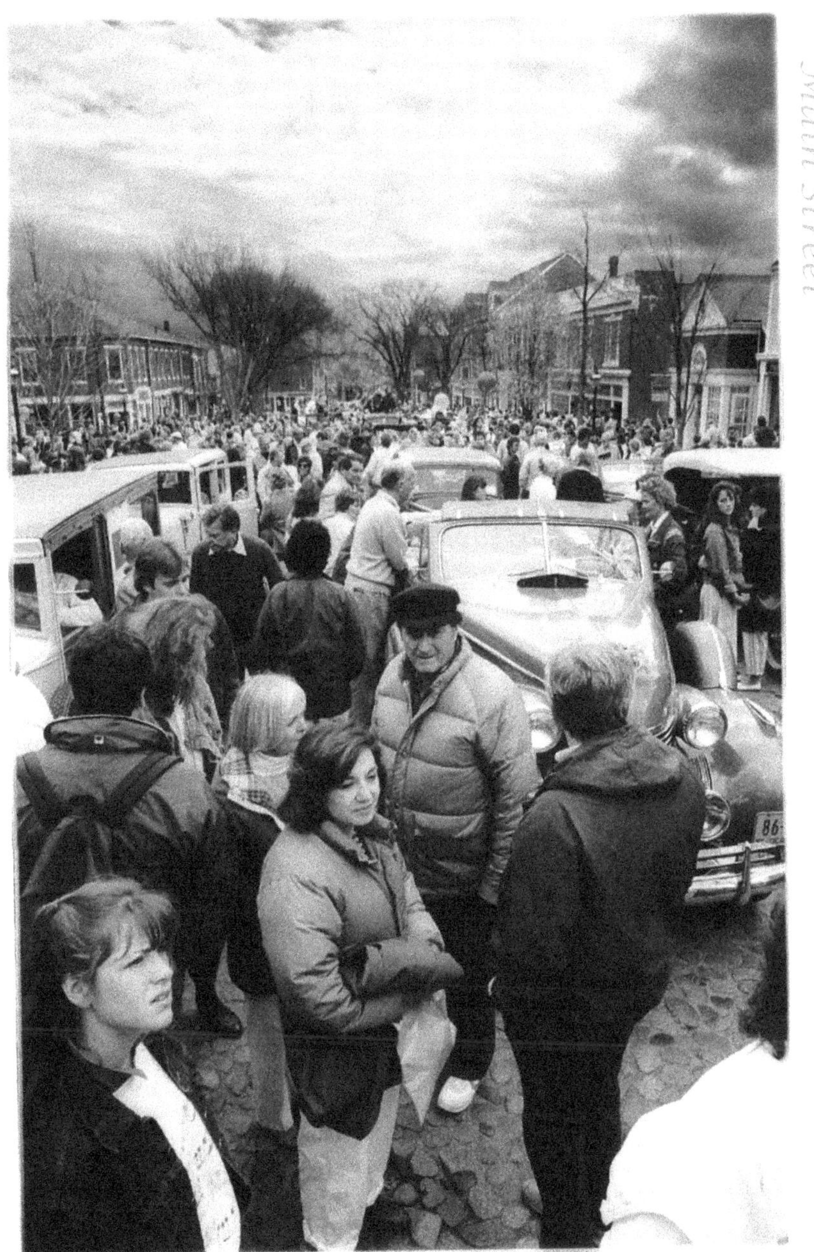

Main Street

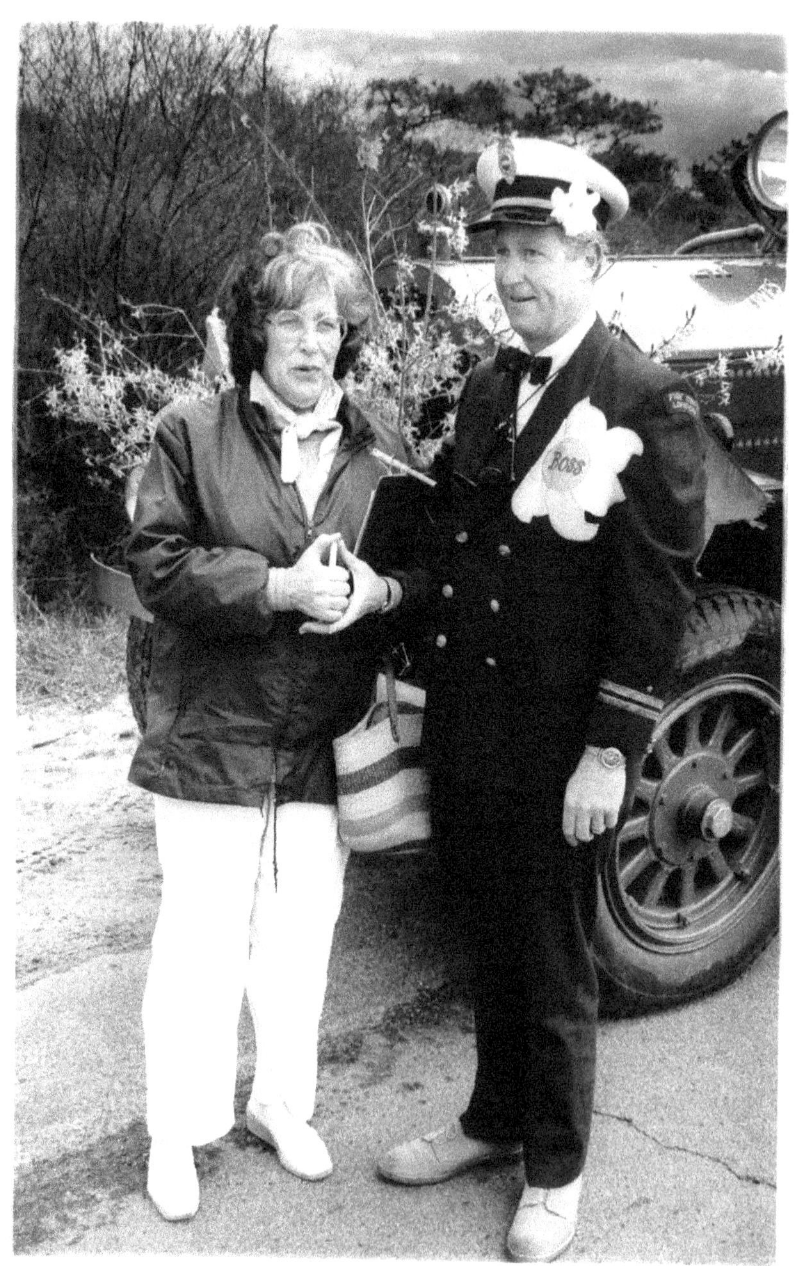
BOSS

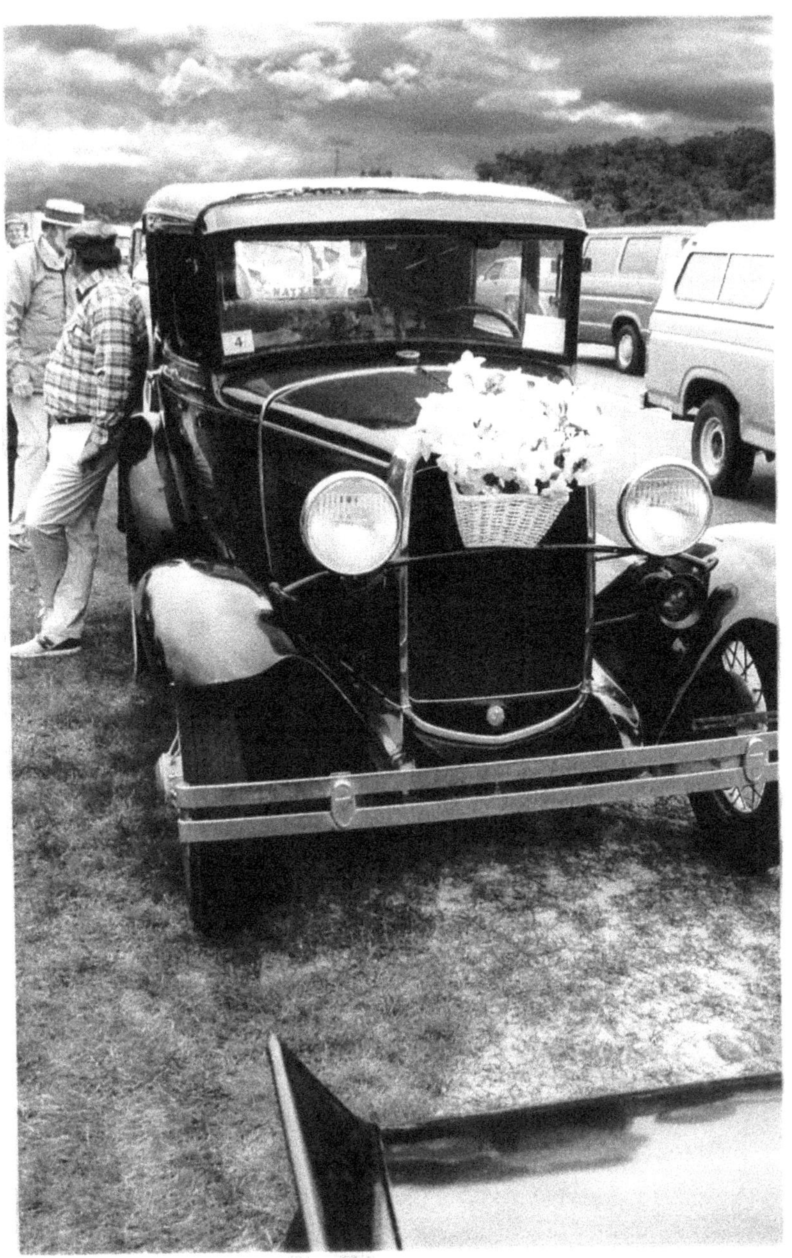

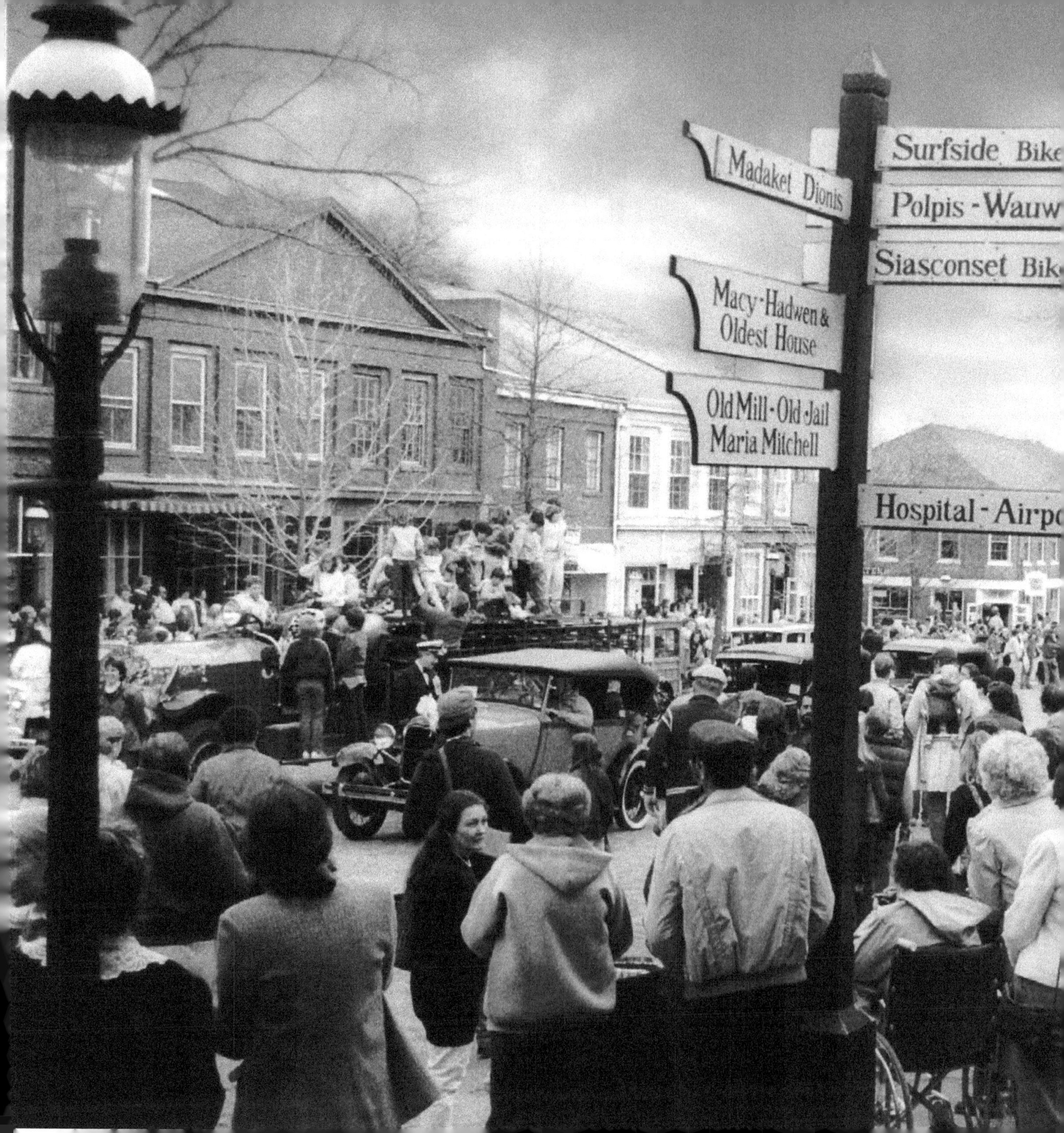
Madaket Dionis
Surfside Bike
Polpis - Wauw
Siasconset Bik
Macy-Hadwen &
Oldest House
Old Mill - Old Jail
Maria Mitchell
Hospital - Airpo

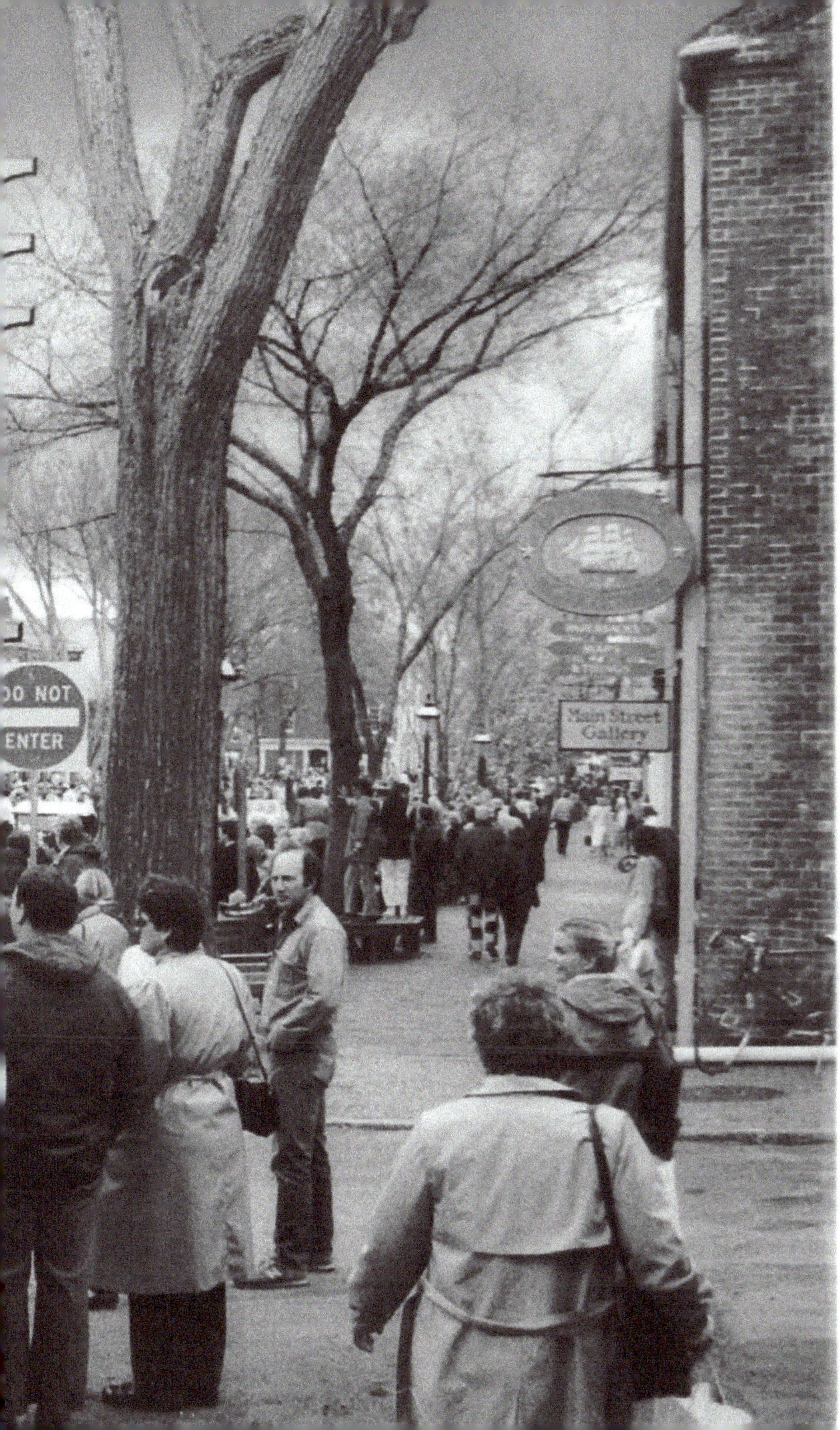

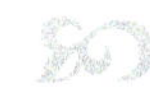

Nantucket Island
Saturday, April 1980

This celebration for the daffodil is more than a mere observance to mark the awakening of spring. It is a testament to the people who live on Nantucket. It is a celebration of their love of life and their love for their island.

I couldn't believe my eyes when I walked to the middle of downtown to be a part of the parade. I stood slack-jawed. So many people that it seemed the cobblestone street had vanished before my very eyes. I've never seen so many people raising such a shout for spring.

The excitement was palpable. It was robust and sweet on my tongue, and I drank it all in—all of it. It was a kaleidoscope of incredible frenzy, vibrating, colors running together into one loud cheer. "Who-la!" Young and old. Mothers, Fathers, brothers, and sisters, enchanted by a simple, sweet flower,

The Trumpet of Spring.

Downtown

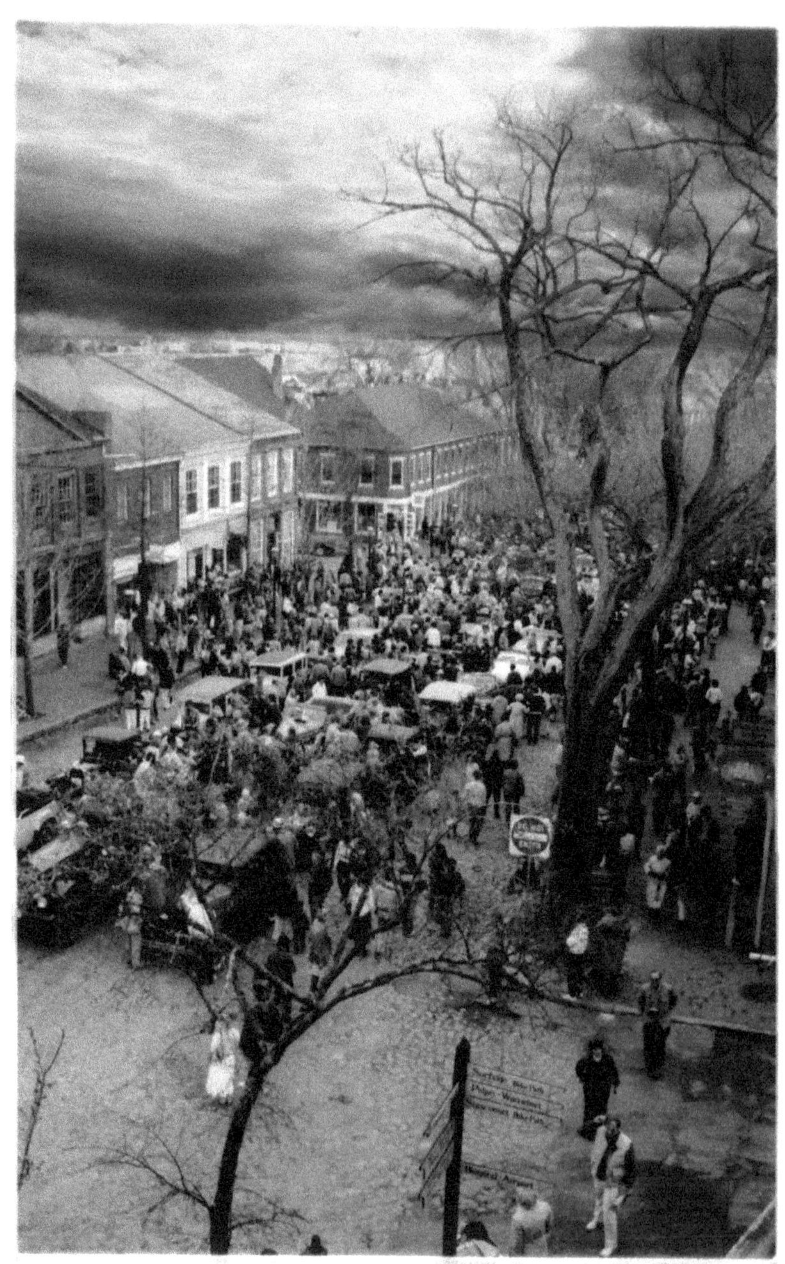

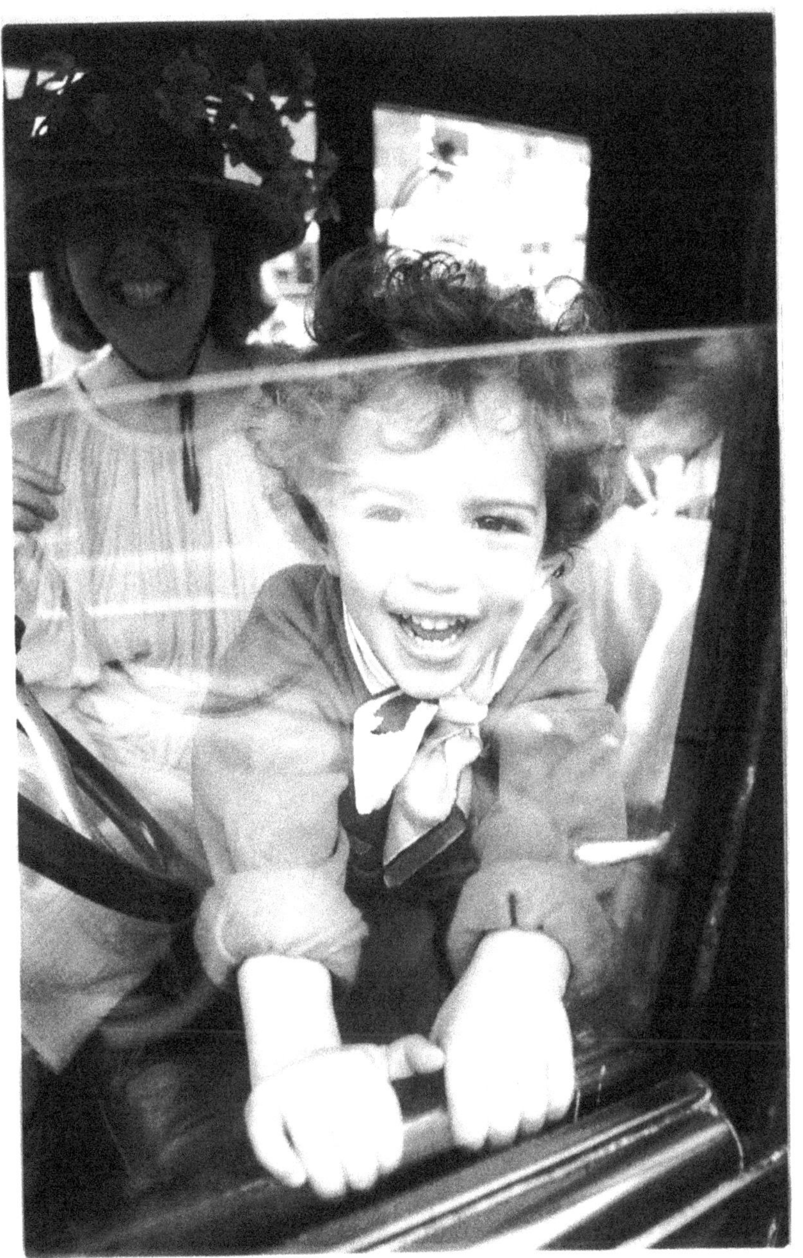

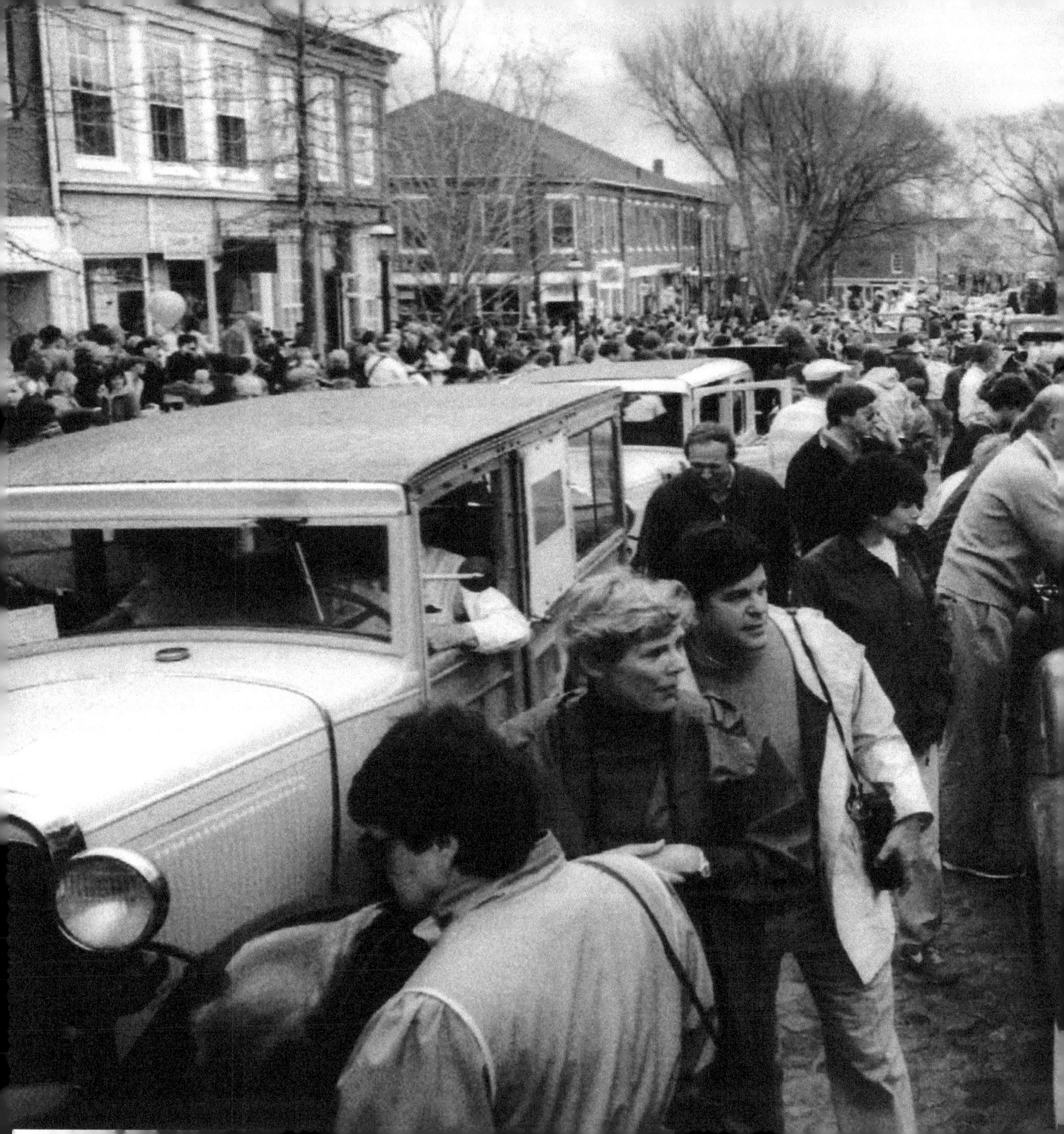

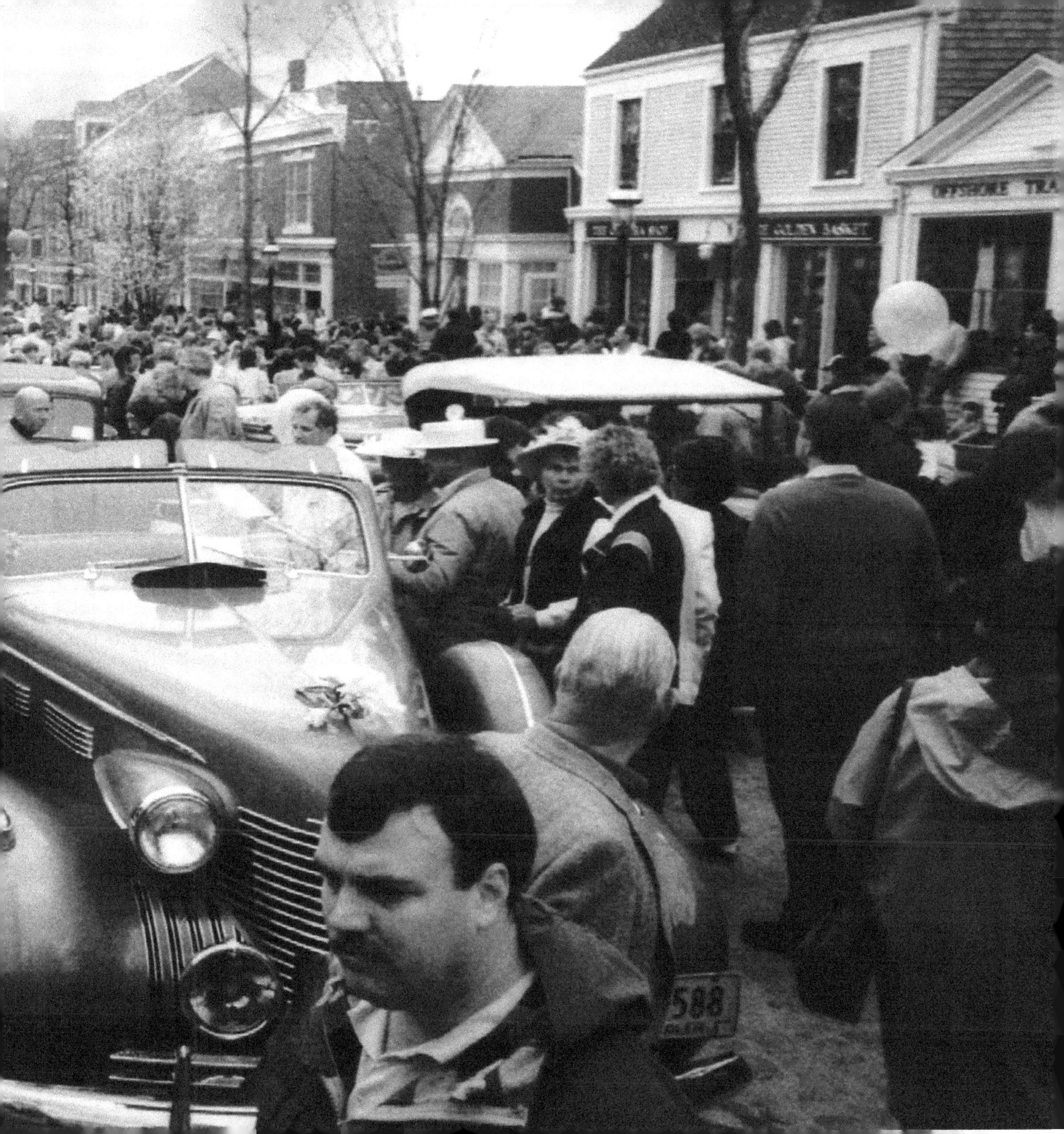
OFFSHORE
588

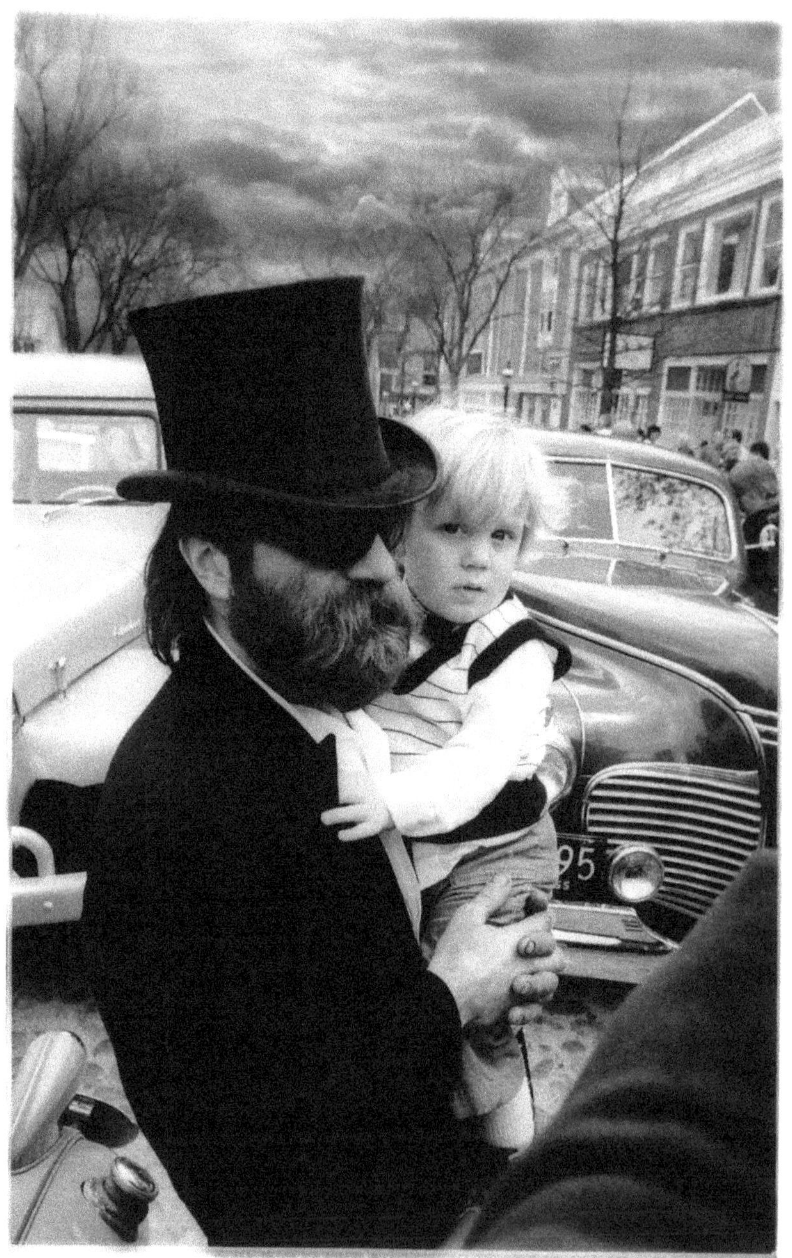

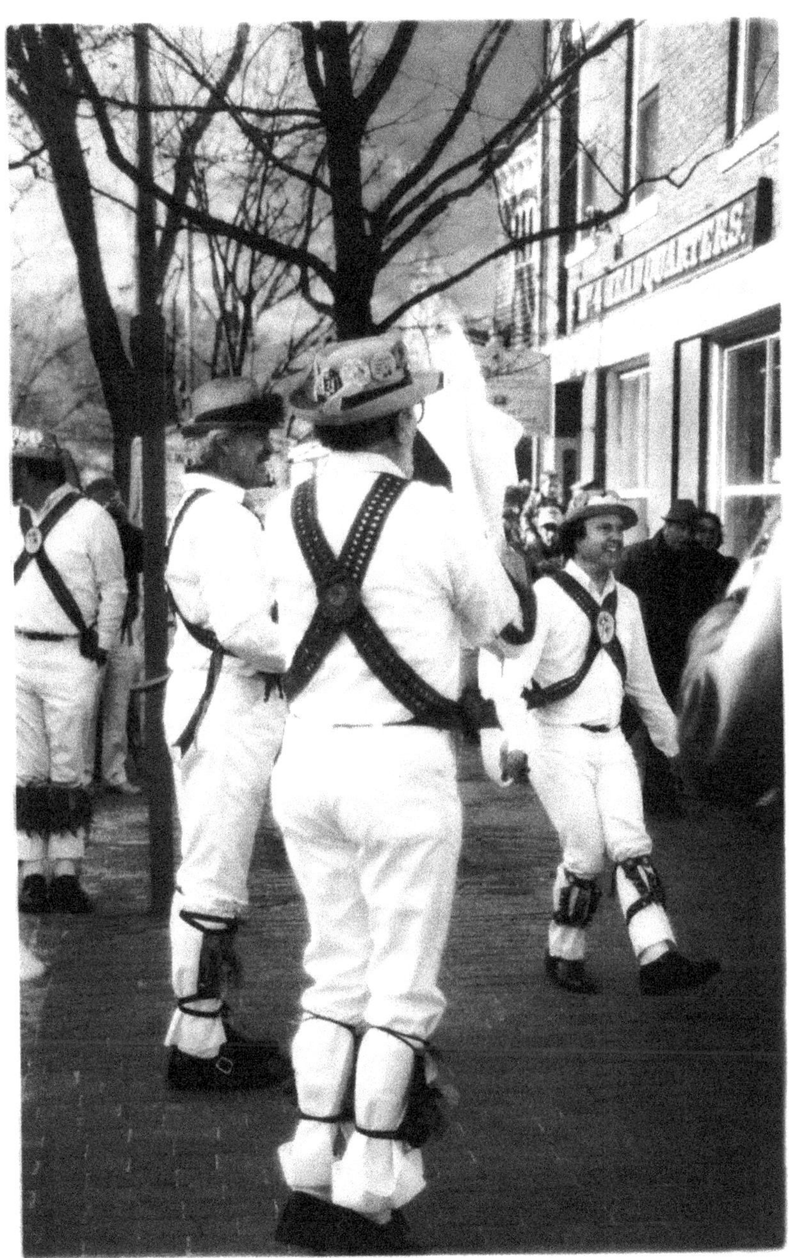

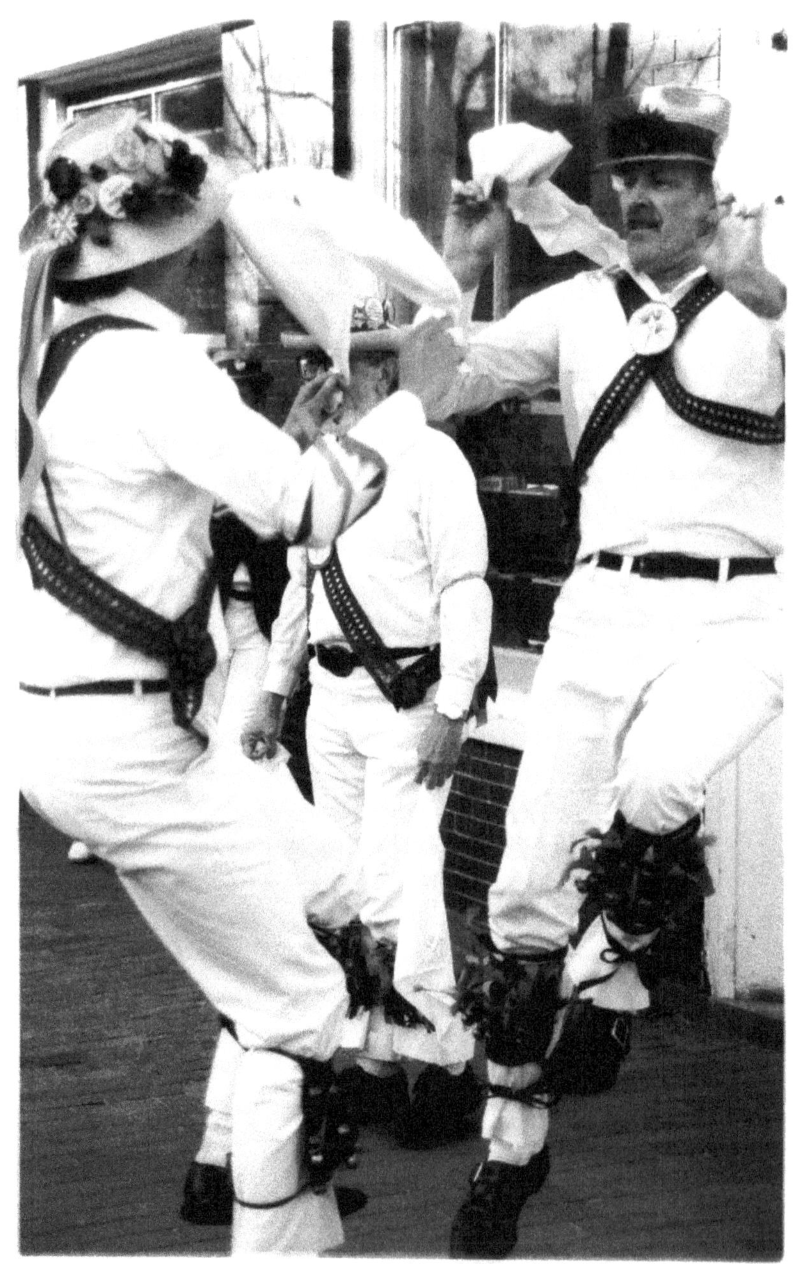

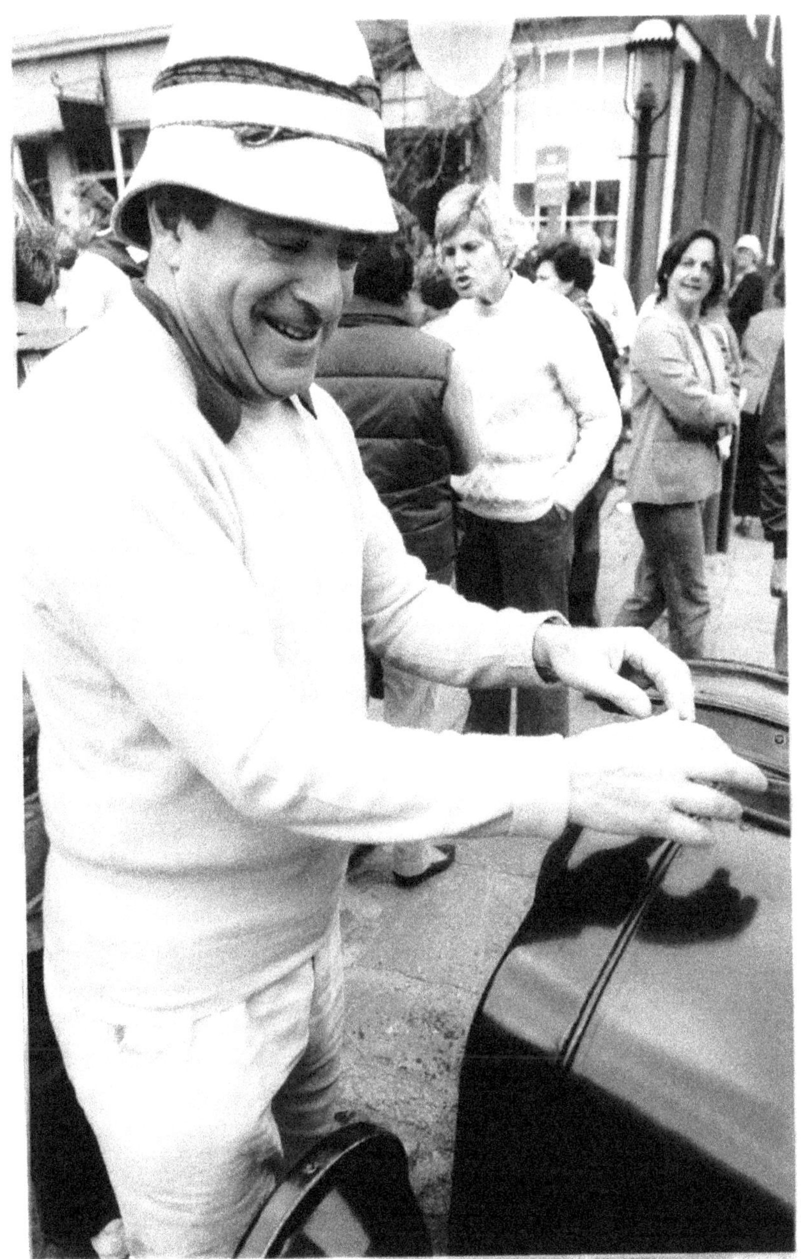

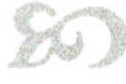

Nantucket Island
Saturday, April 1980

This, the 6th Daffodil Jamboree will be a festivity that will last for decades, no doubt about it. I can just imagine the size of the crowd one hundred years from now.

And as I mingled in and around the phalanx of people, a thought bounced around inside my head like good ole fashioned churned butter and made me laugh.

Why, they would be forced to stop the running of the ferries and close Hyannis Port with a huge sign that read,

"Sorry. Nantucket is full. Try again tomorrow."

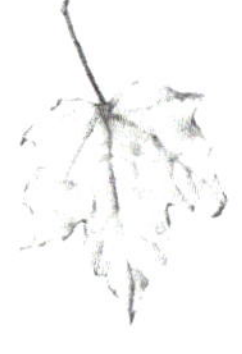

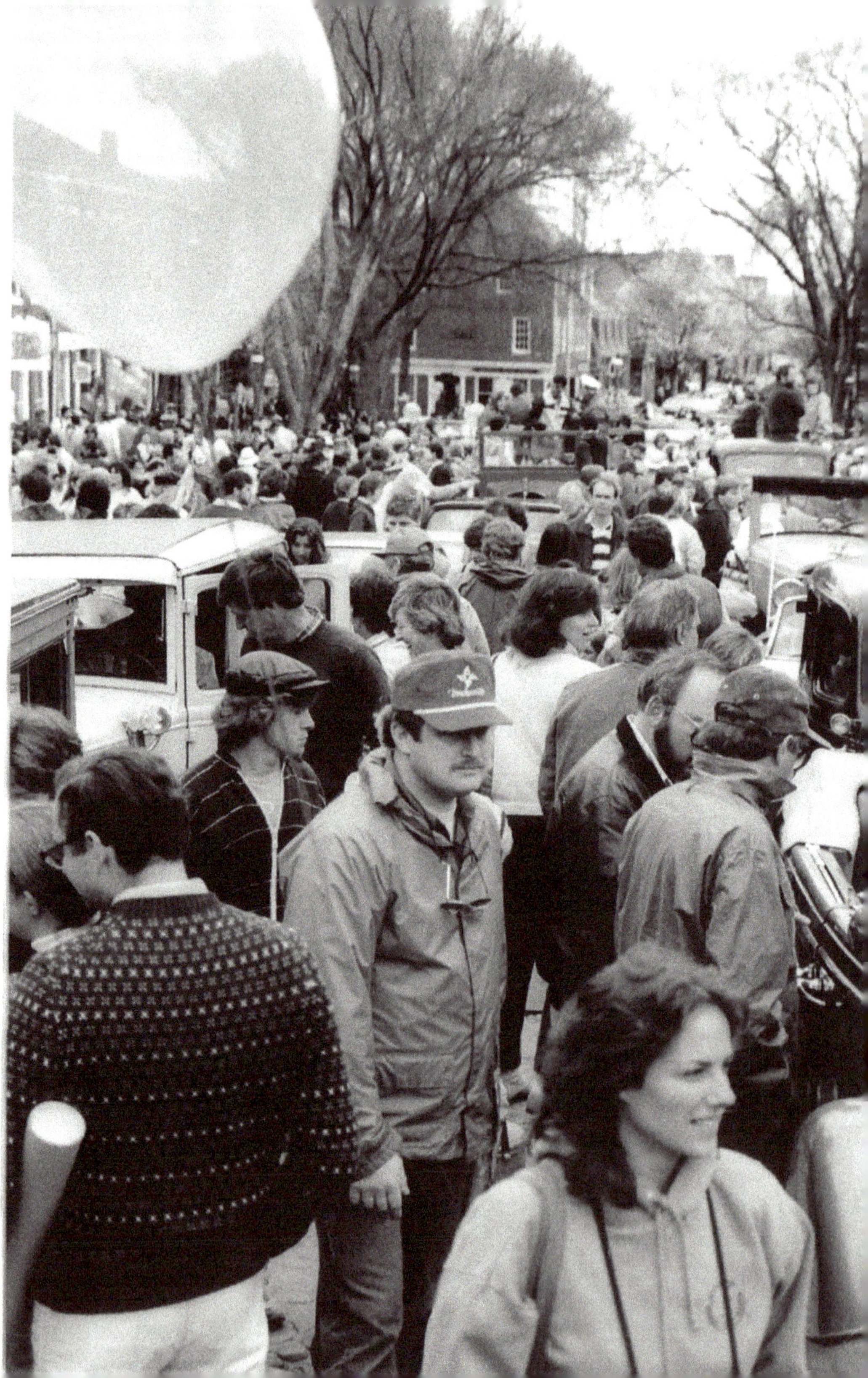

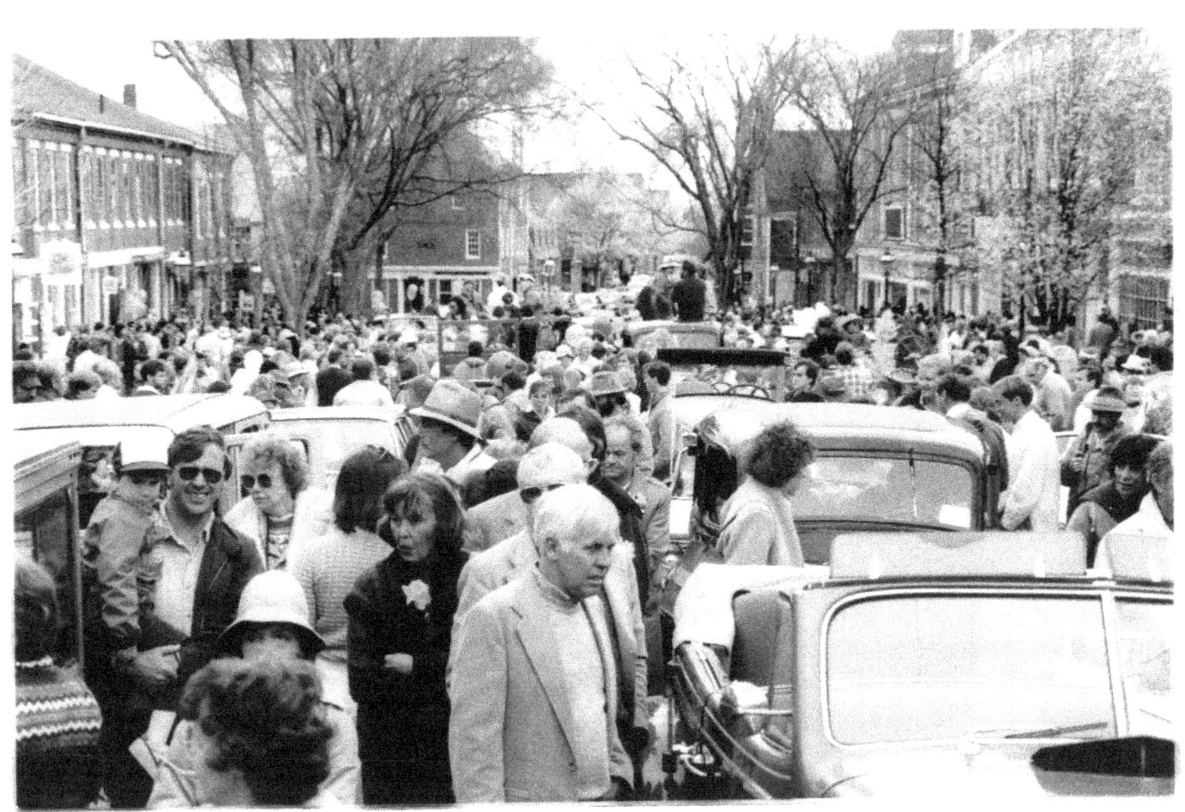

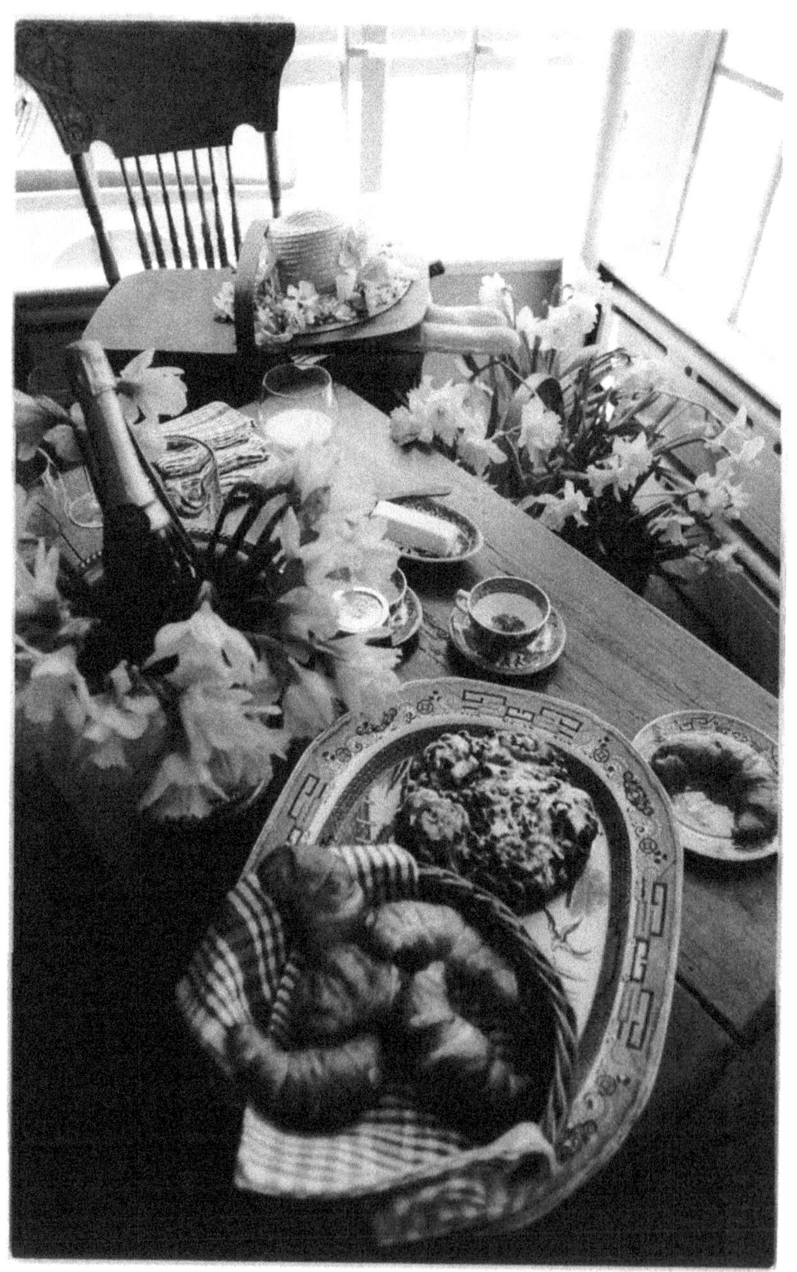

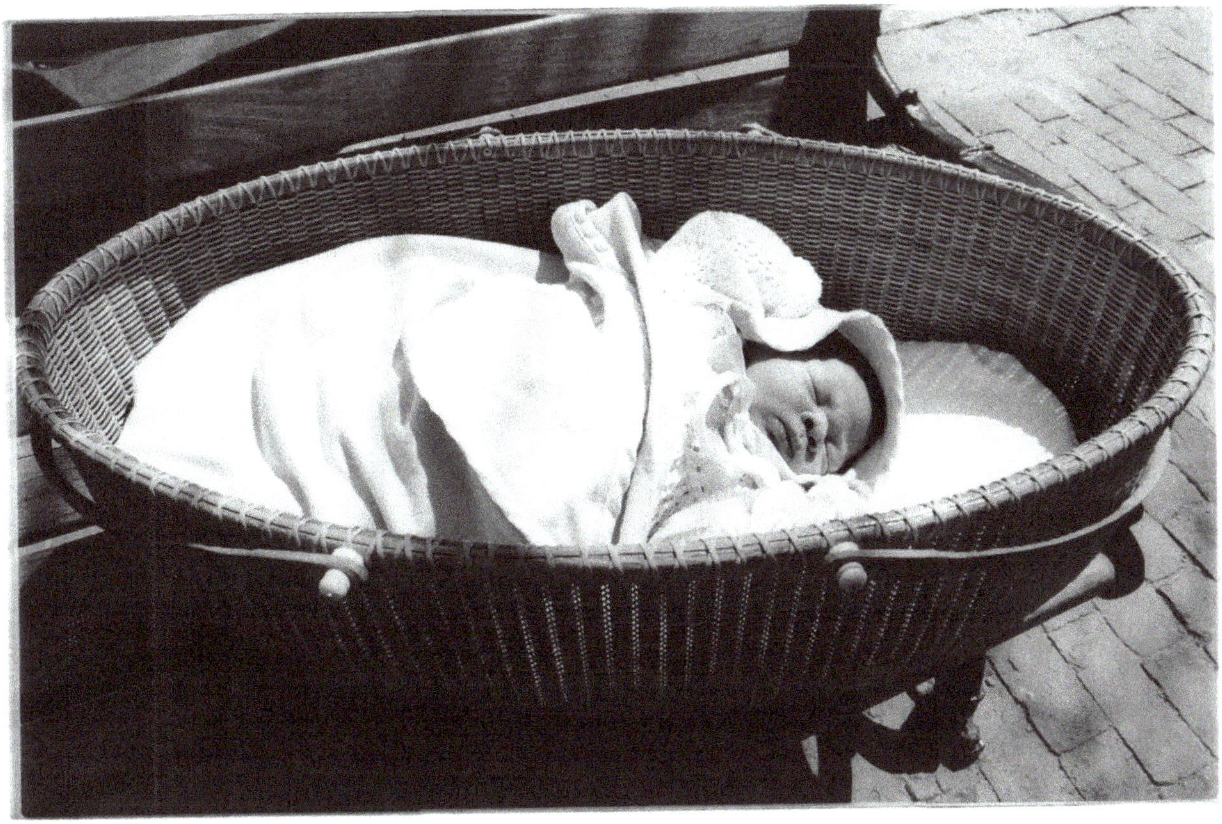

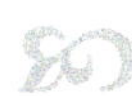

Nantucket Island
Saturday, April 1980
Early Evening. What an amazing day. So many people and the classic and antique cars! Not to mention all the food . . . I was in heaven.

Babies ferried, nestled all snug in lightship baskets. Shop windows decorated with yellow dancing flowers, waiting to be chosen best of the show. Restaurant tables garnished with the same buttery delight. Picnics, lavish and simple in the trunks of cars. Everywhere daffodils and more daffodils to bring smiles to everyone's soul.

Hurrah, hurrah. Hurrah for spring. I say, "Hip-hip-hurrah!"

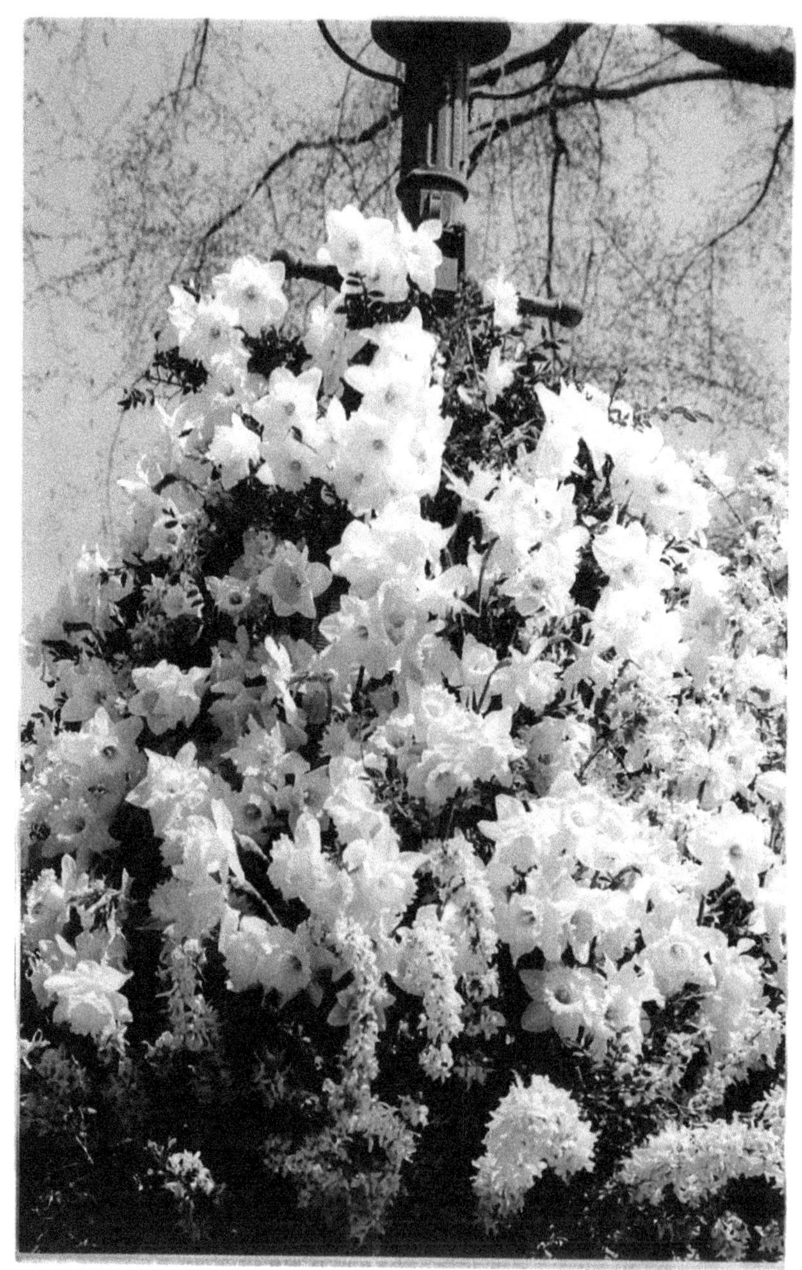

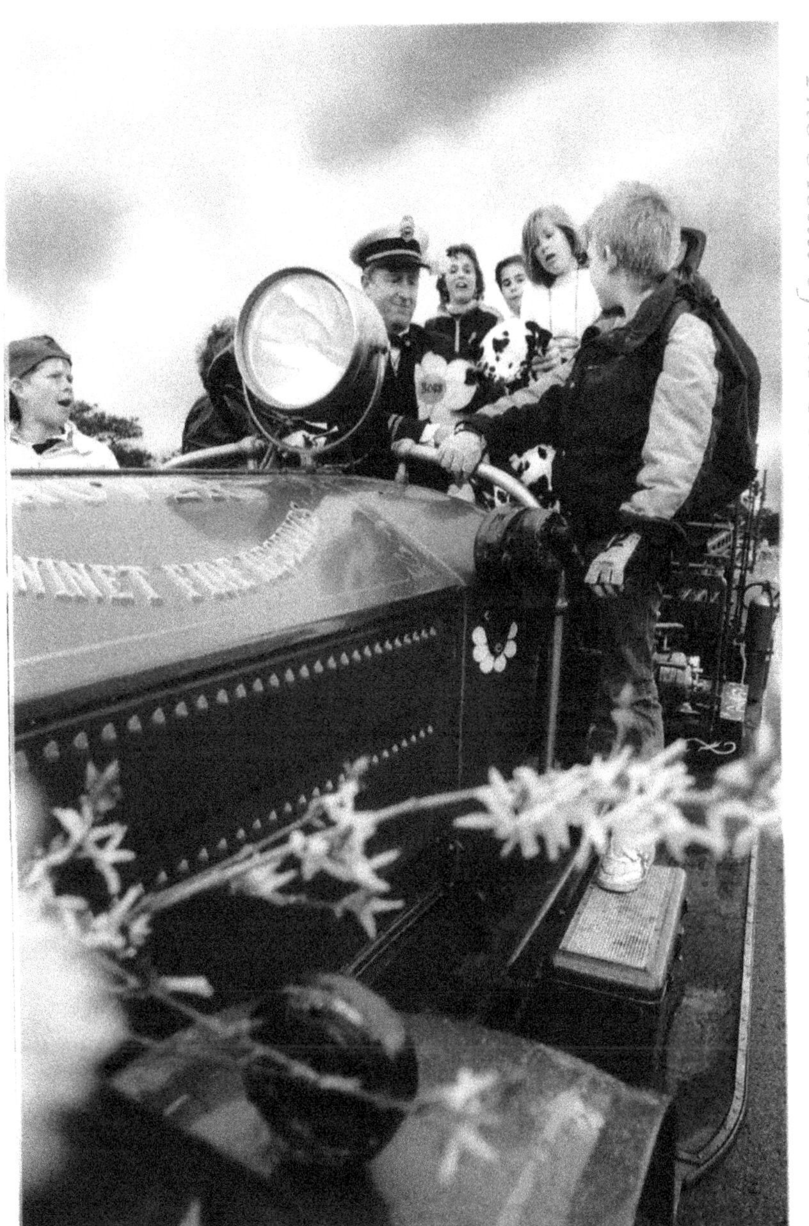

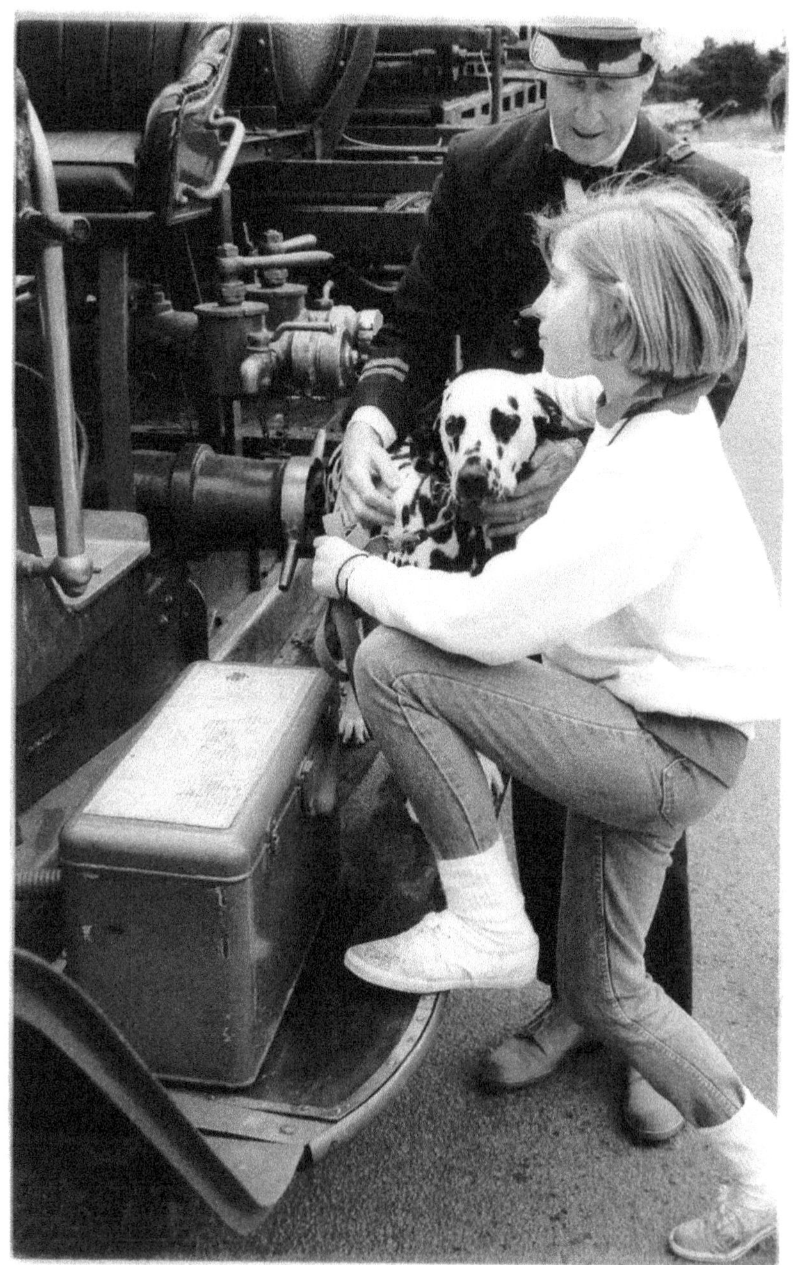

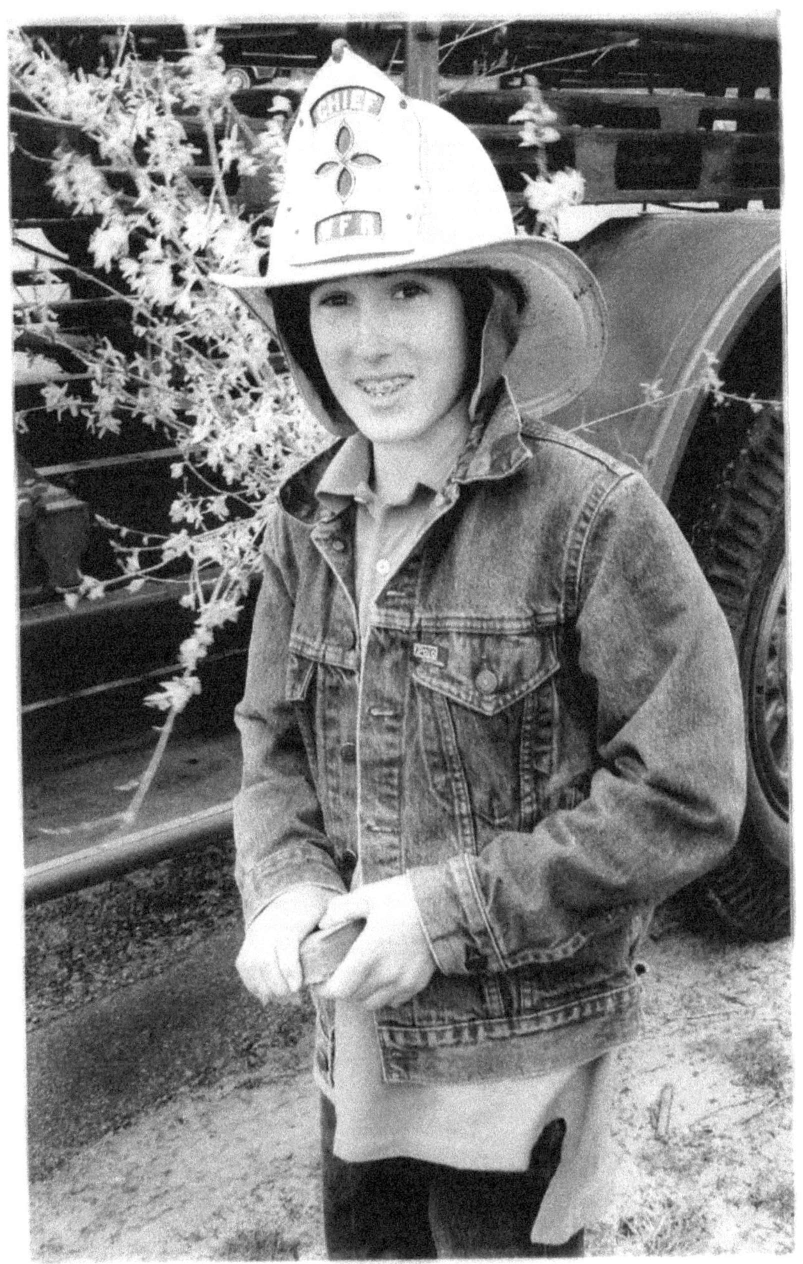

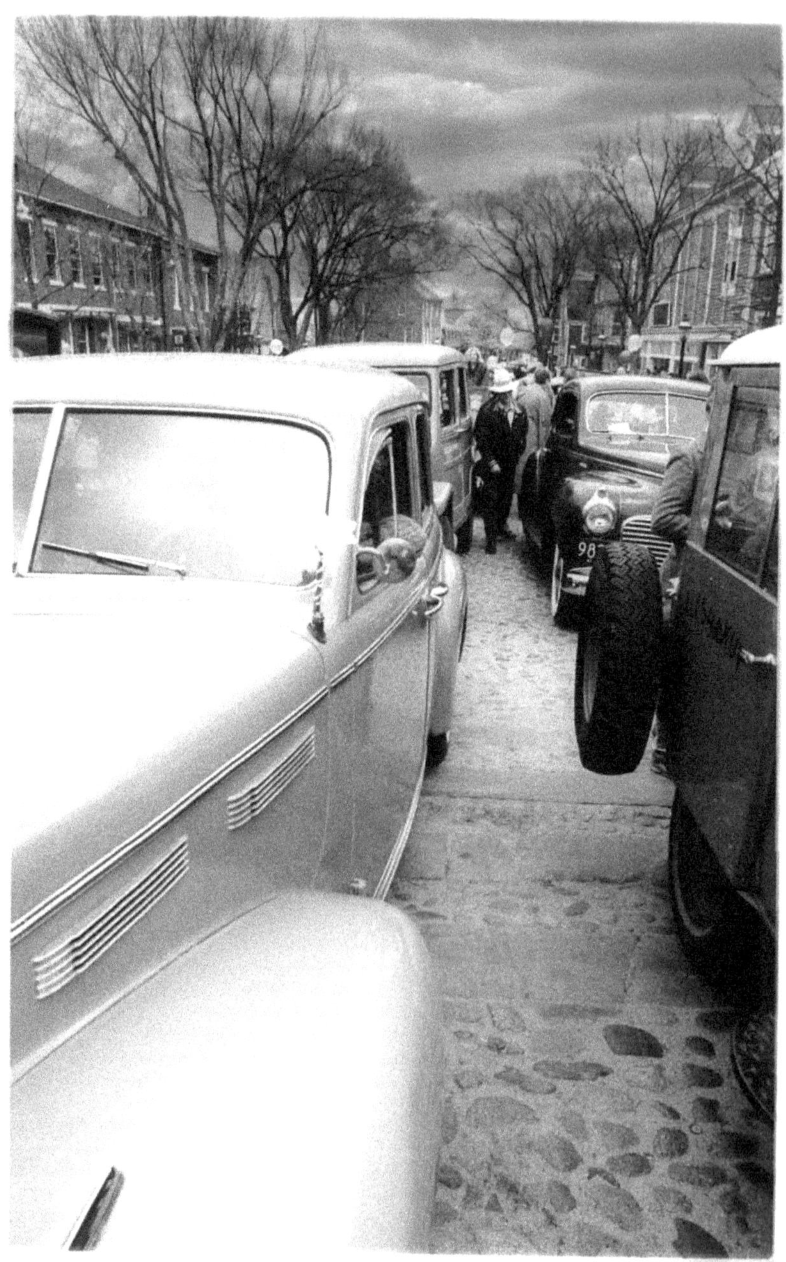

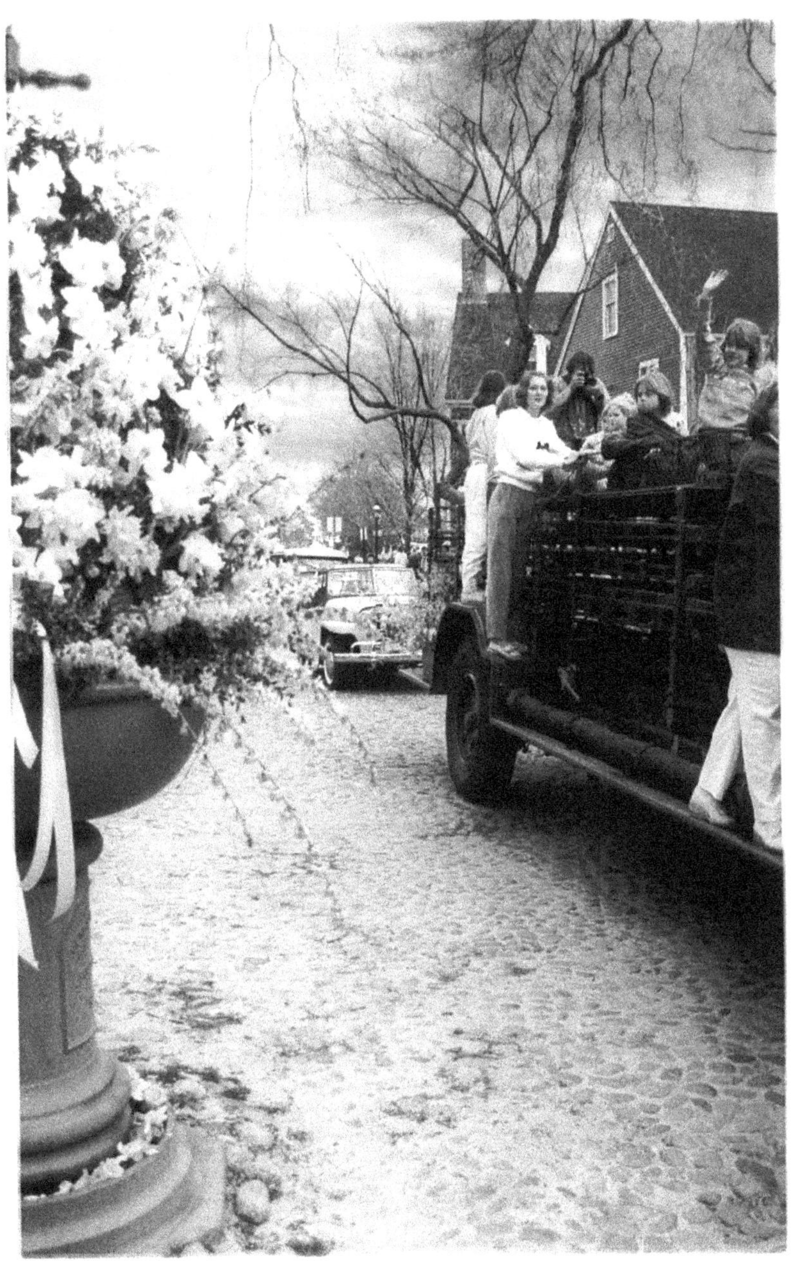

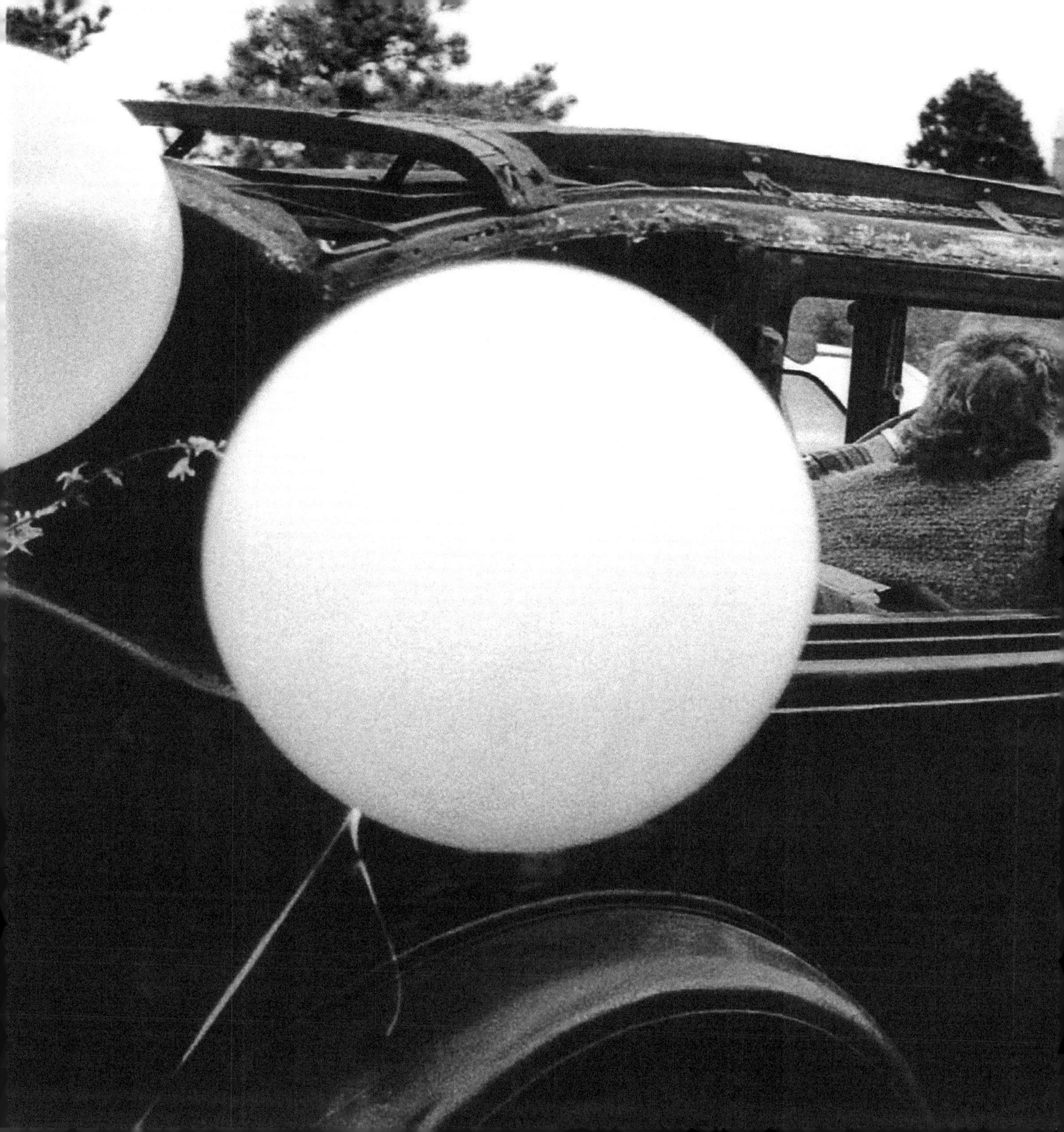

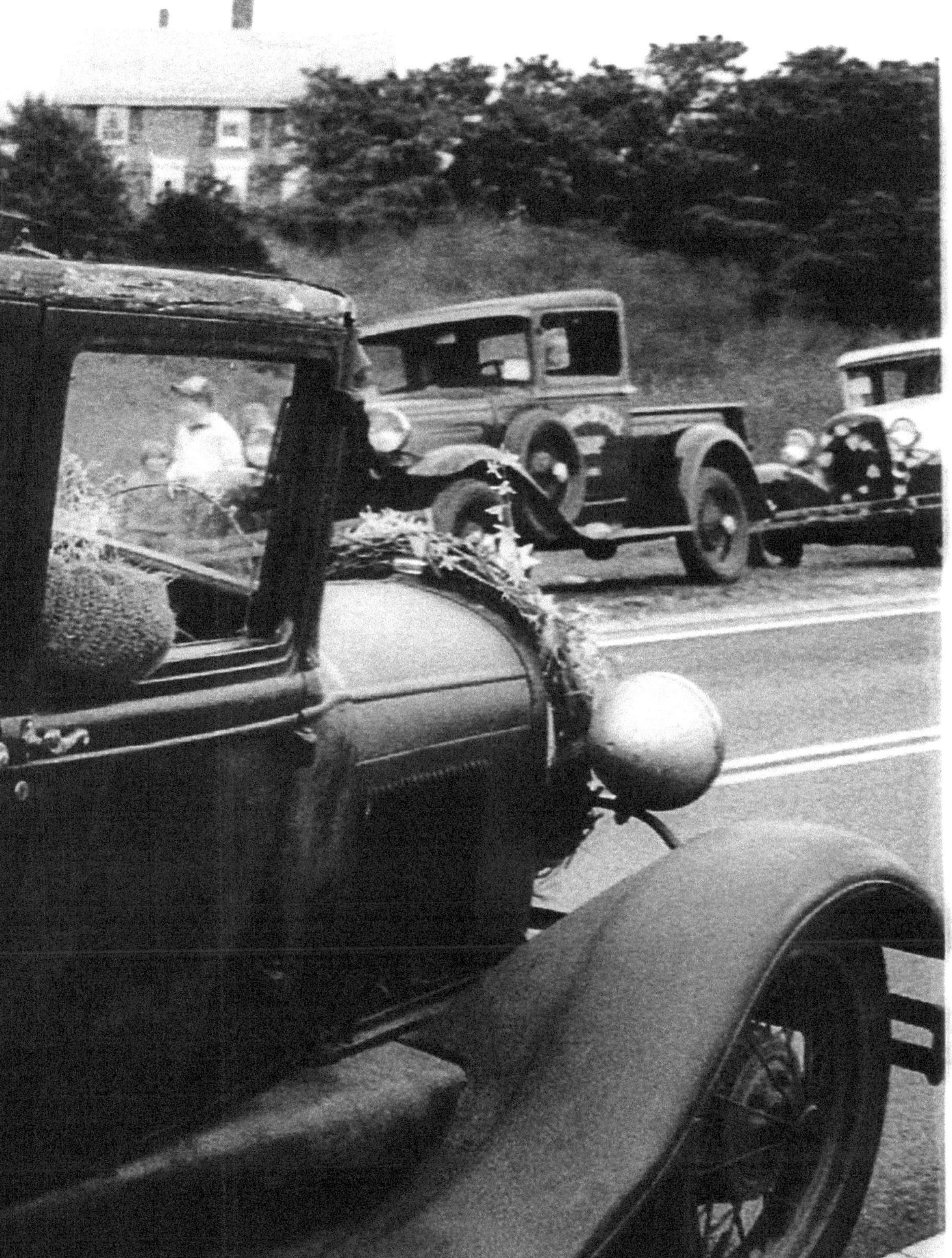

Driving Along Milestone Road to Siasconset

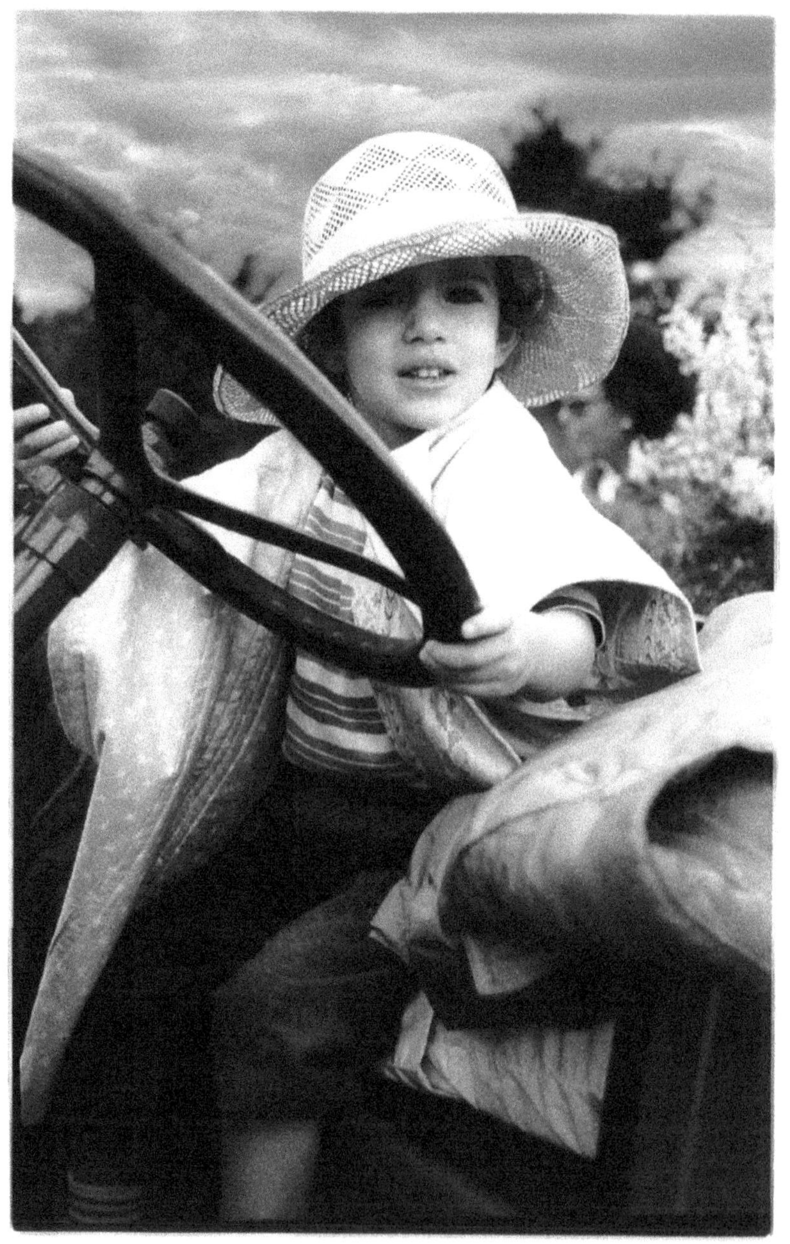

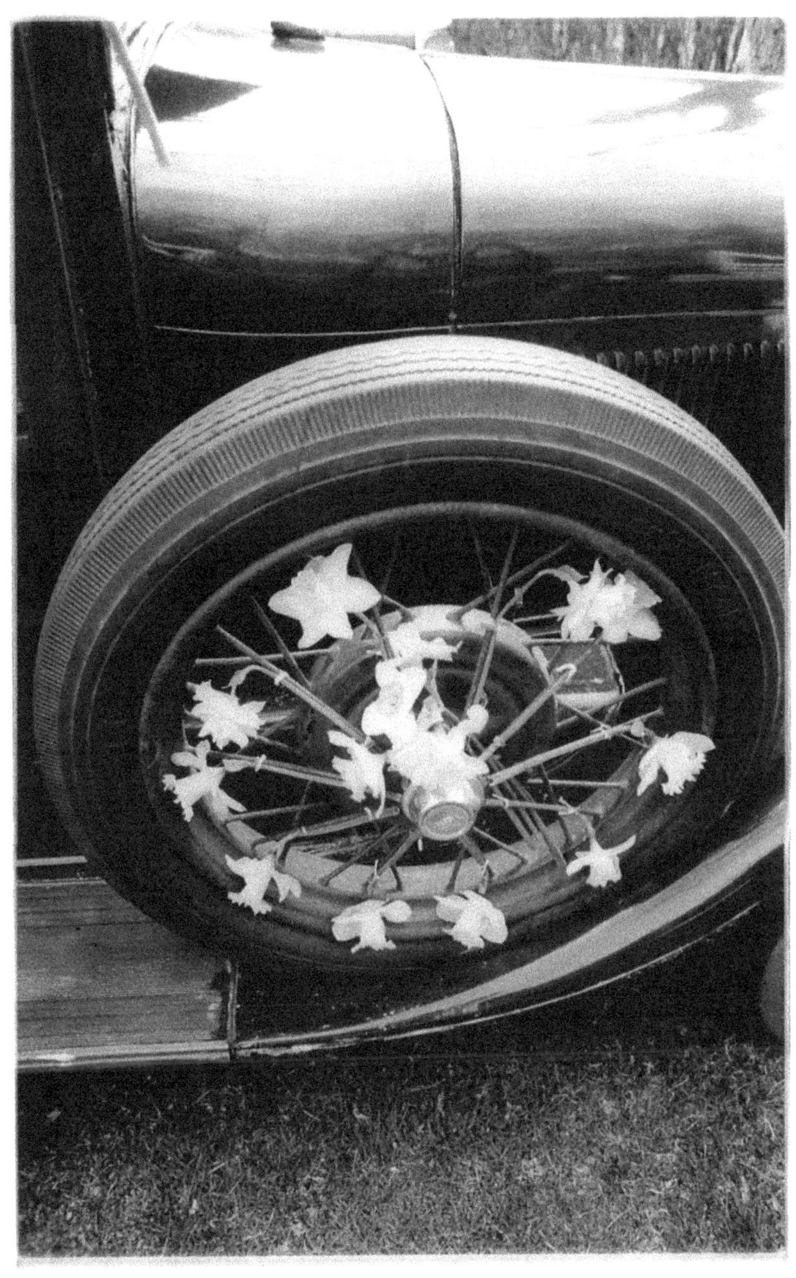

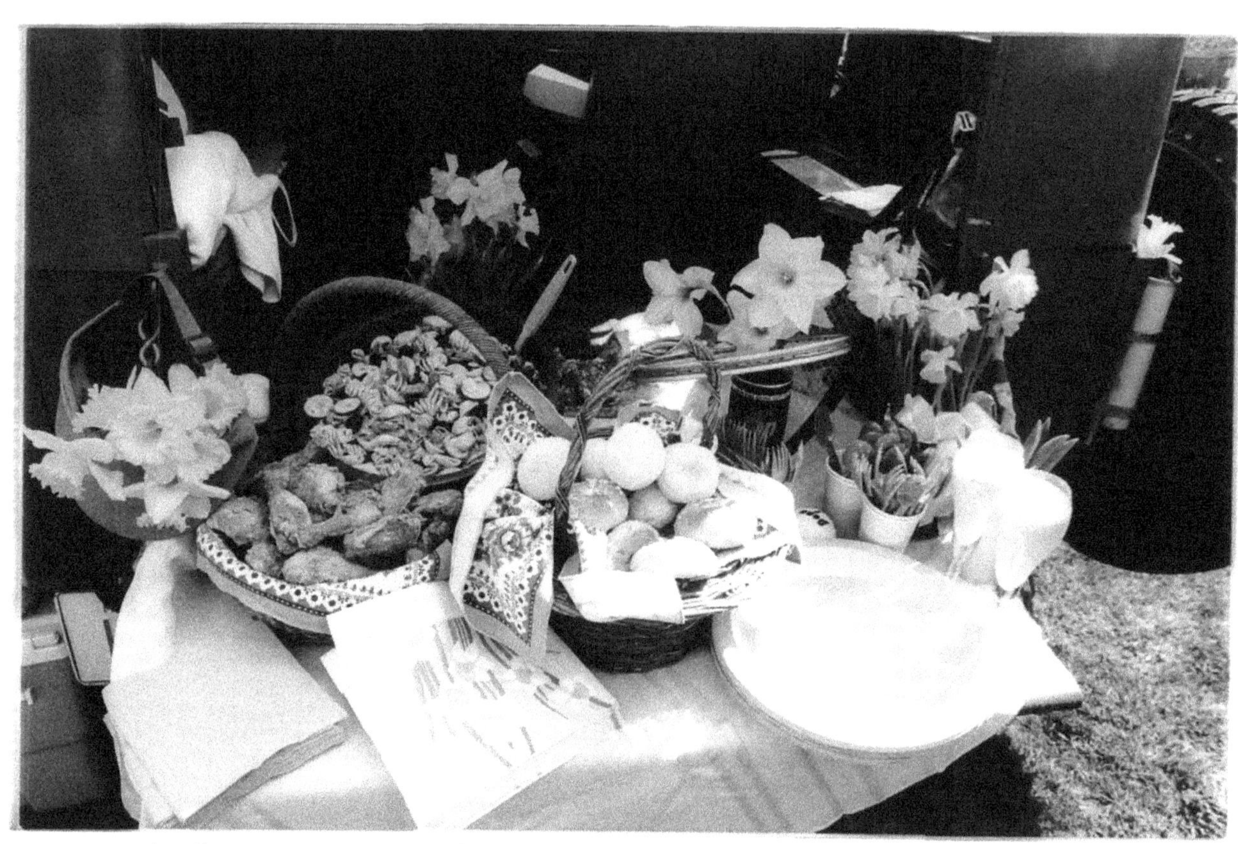

Tailgating, Car Show and Picnicking - Siasconset

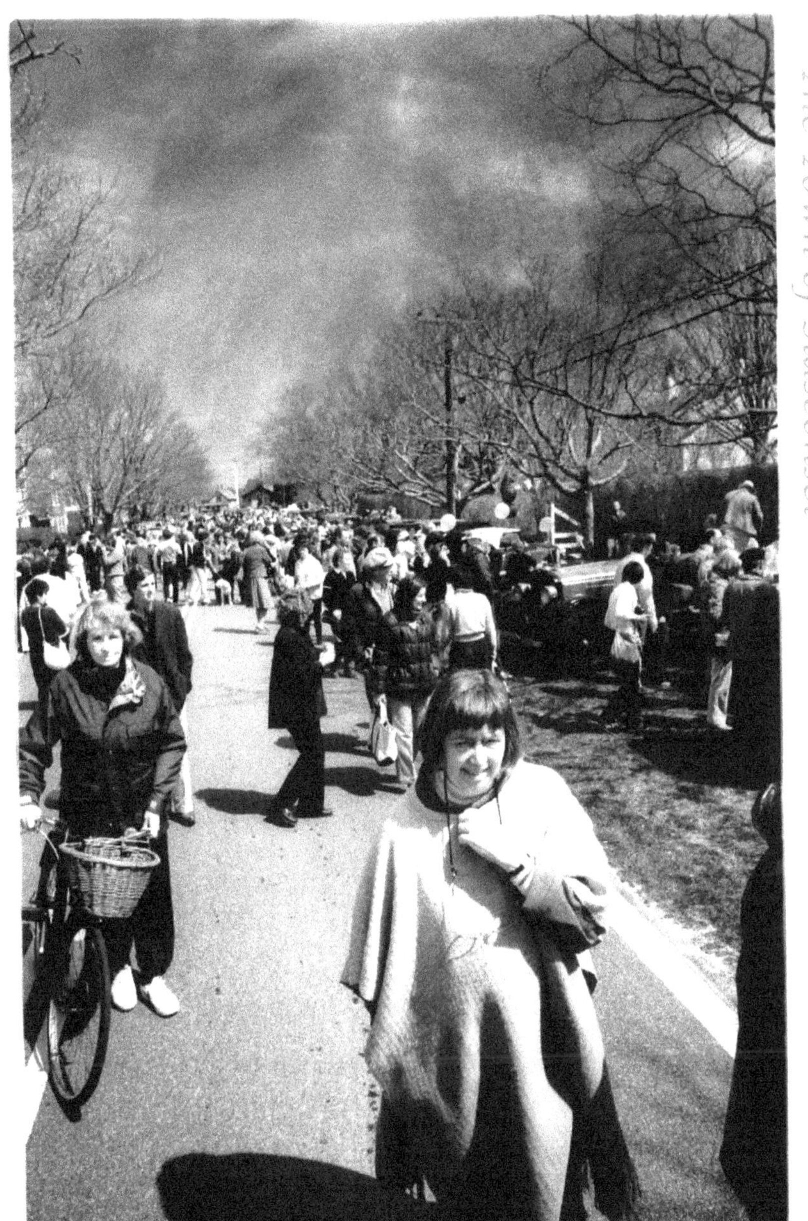

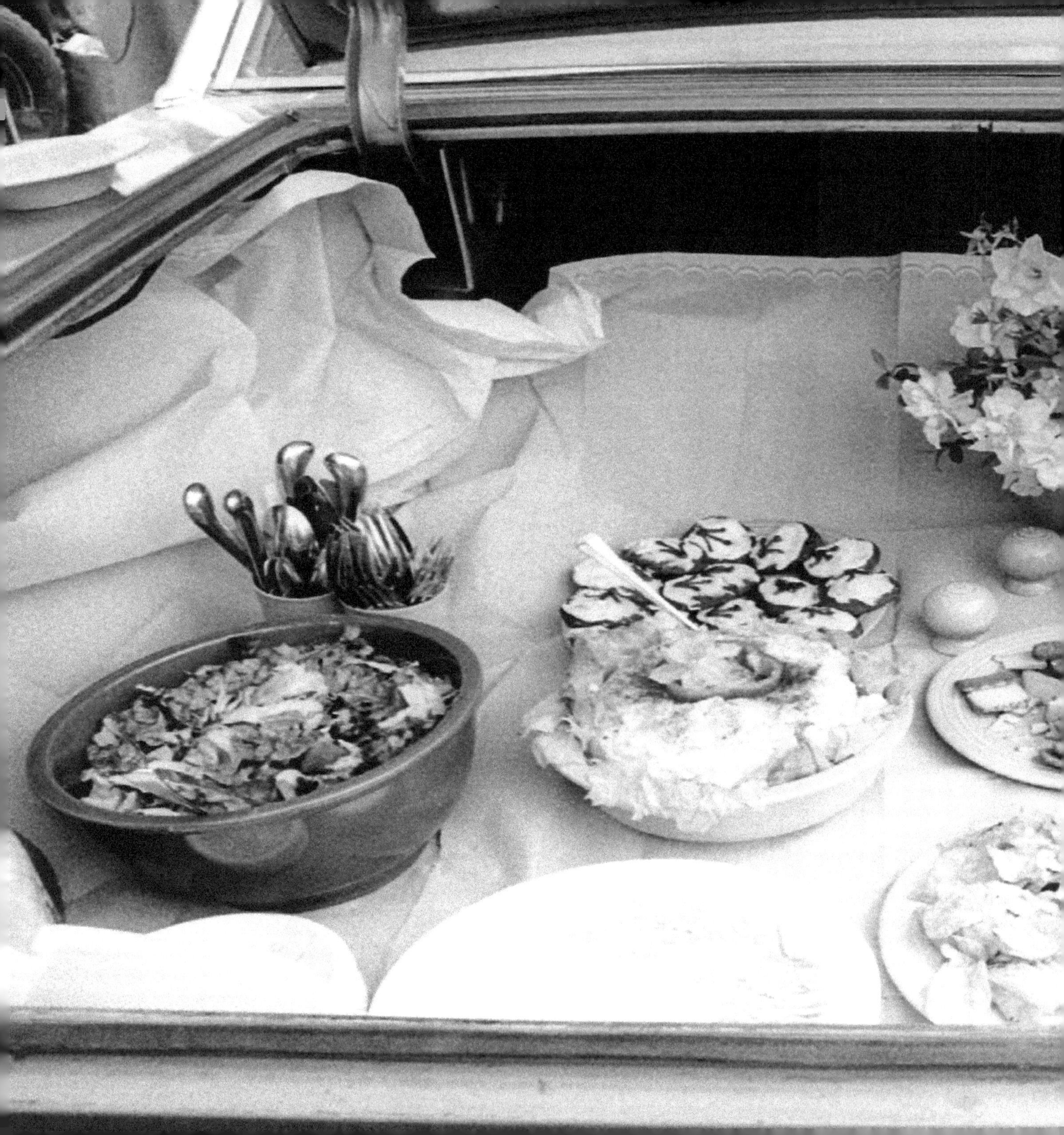

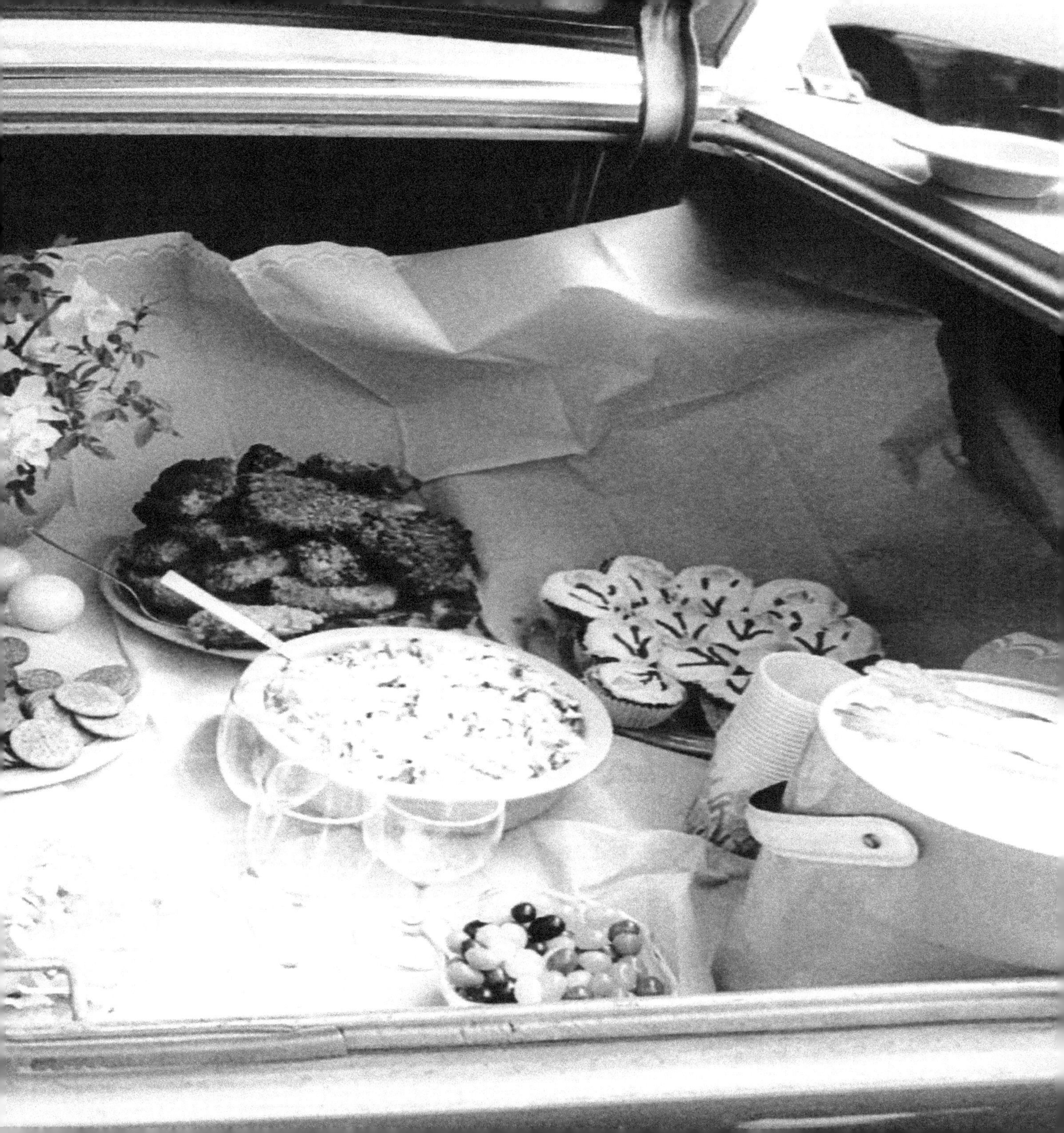

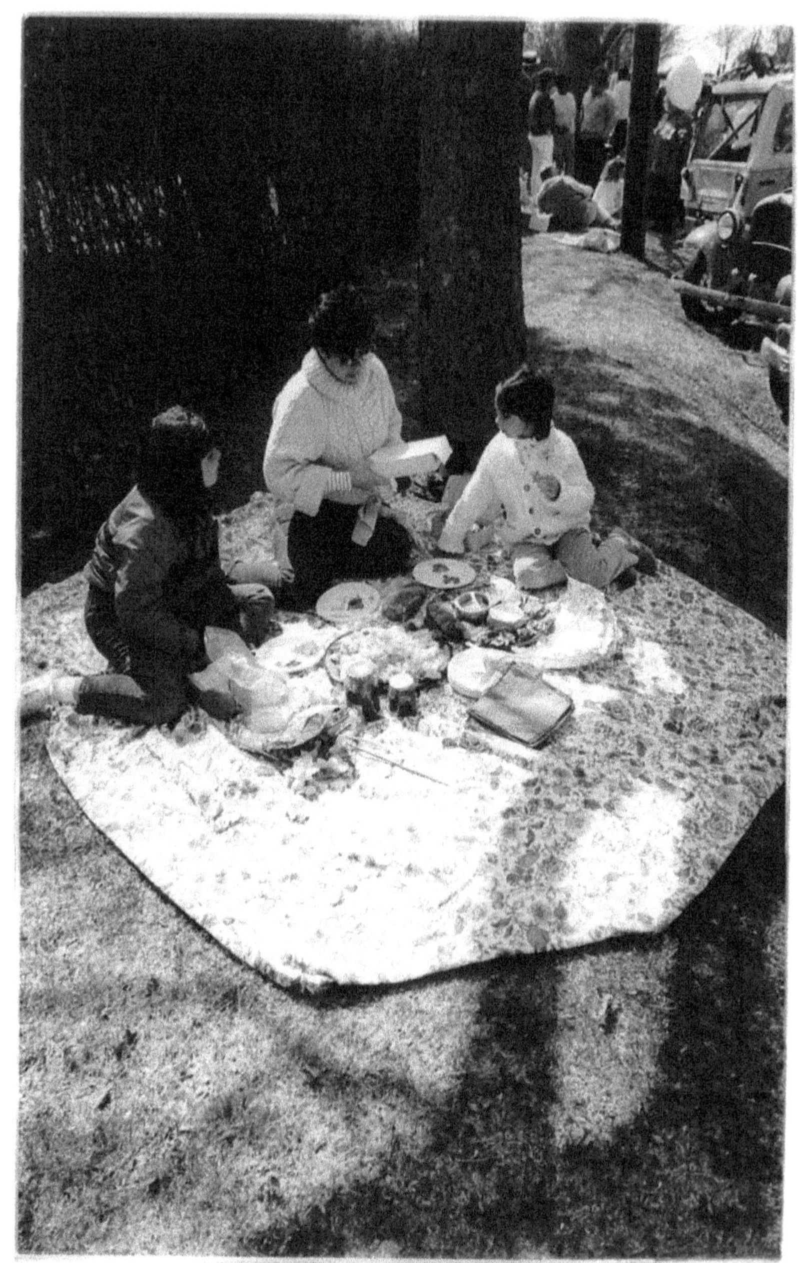

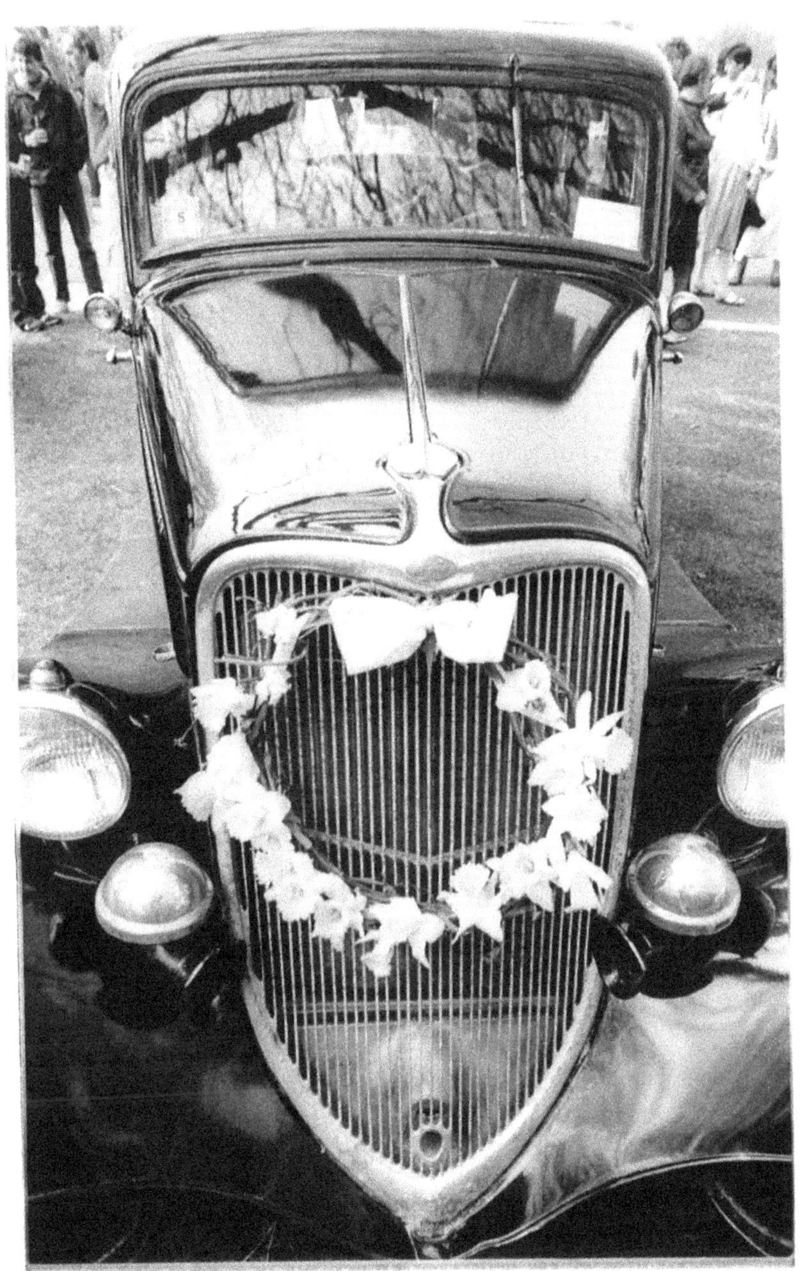

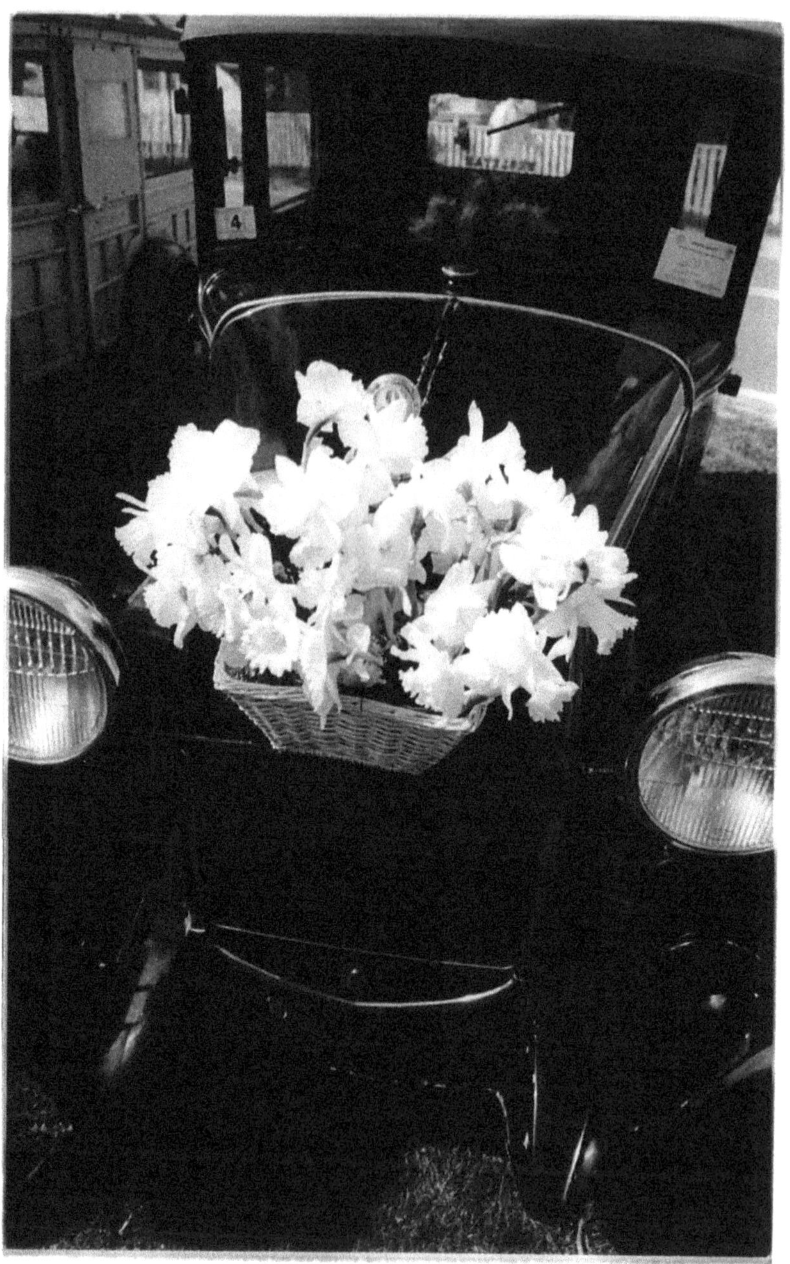
4

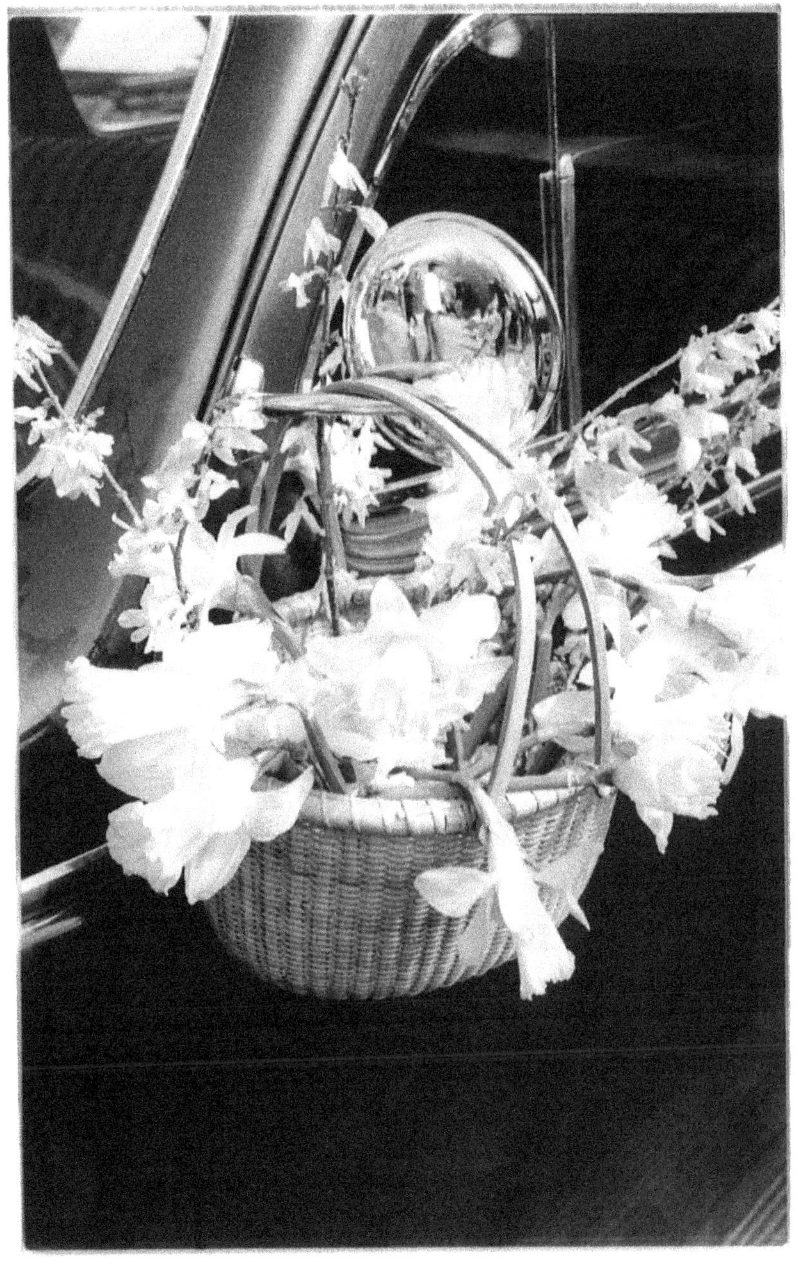

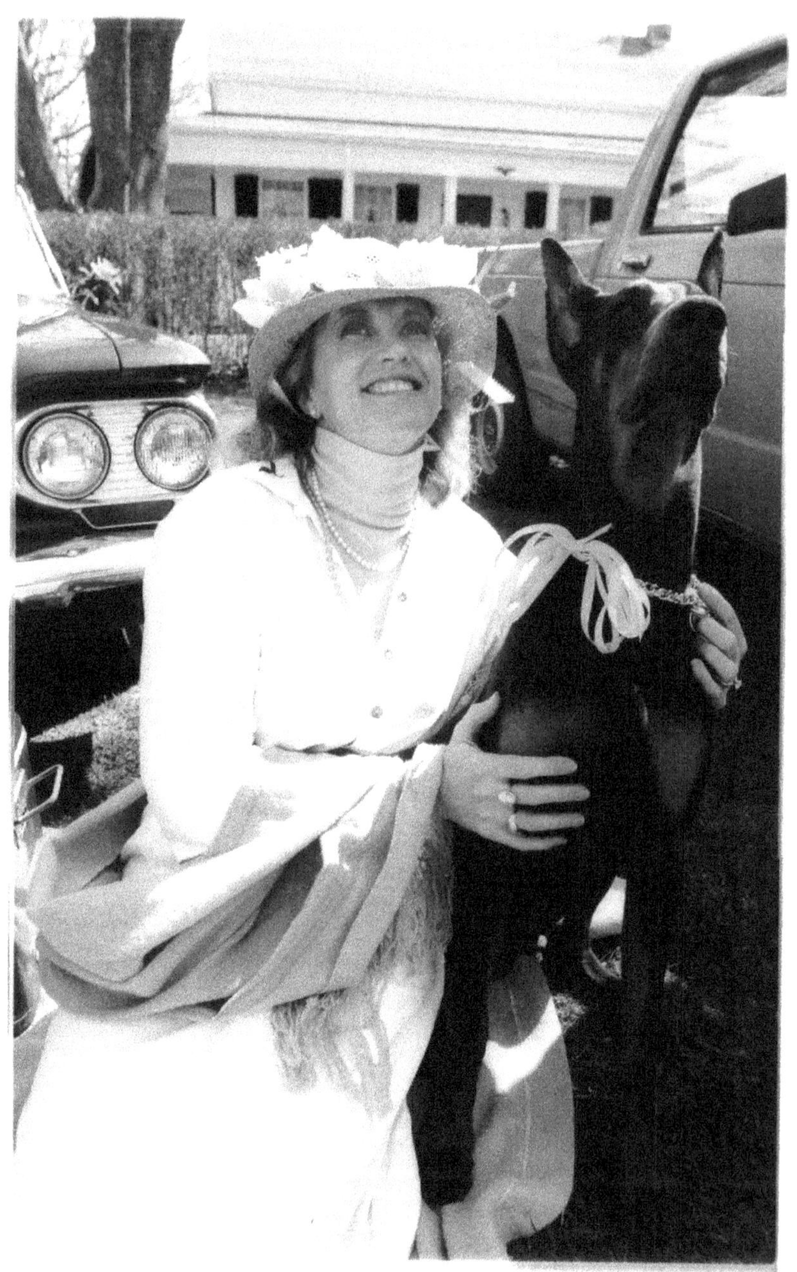

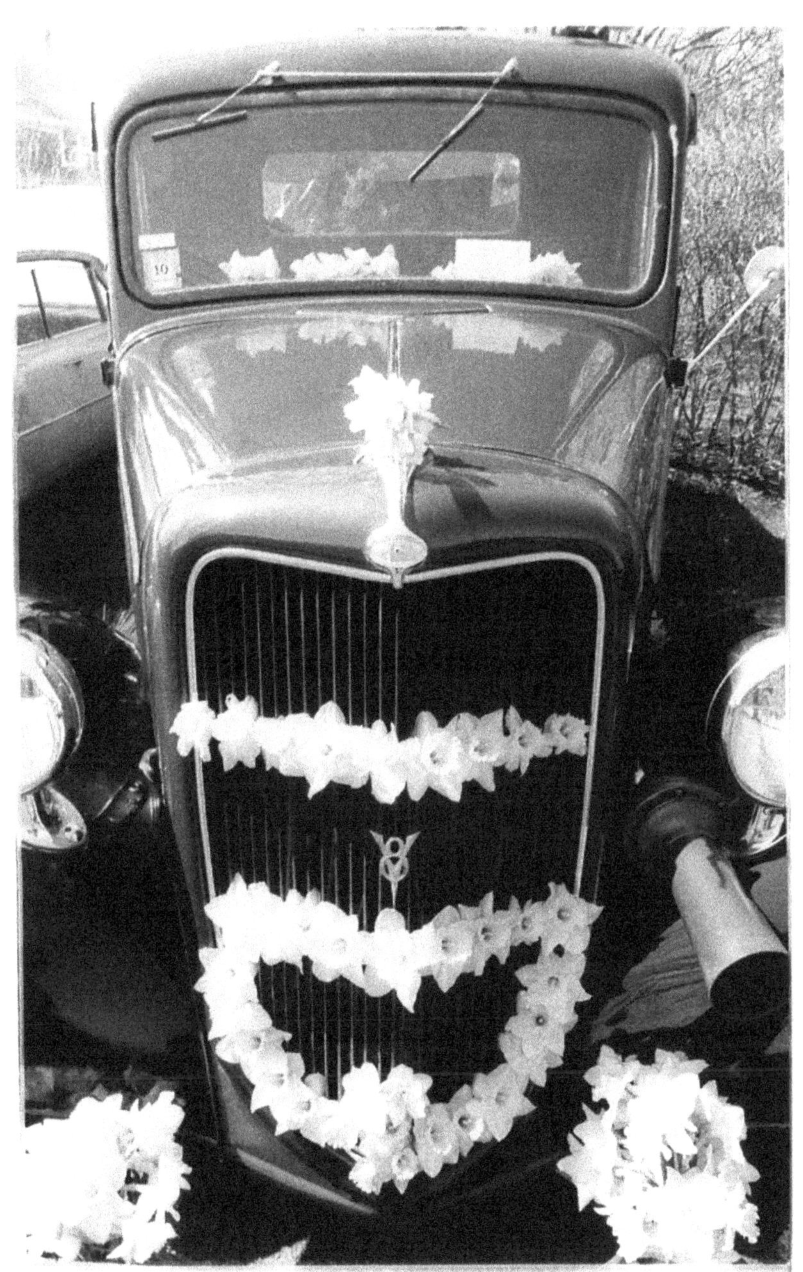

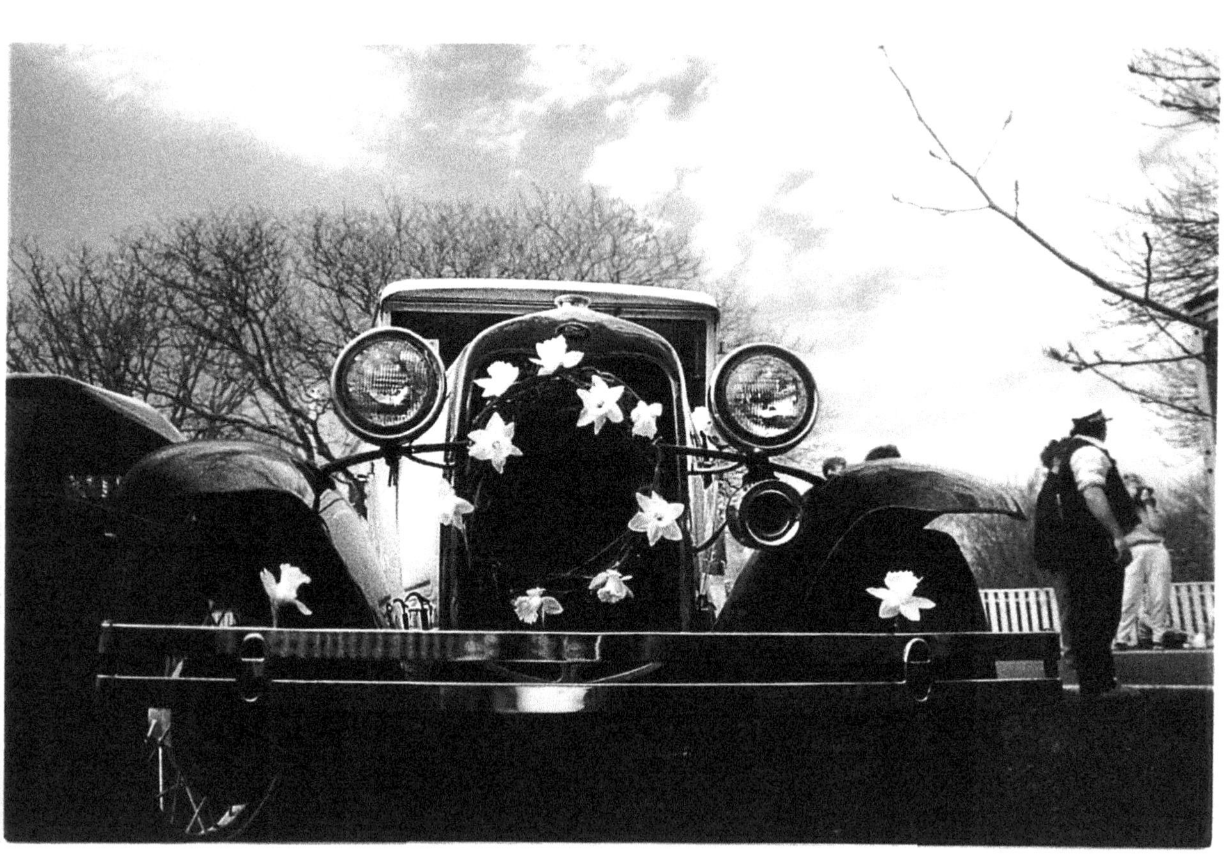

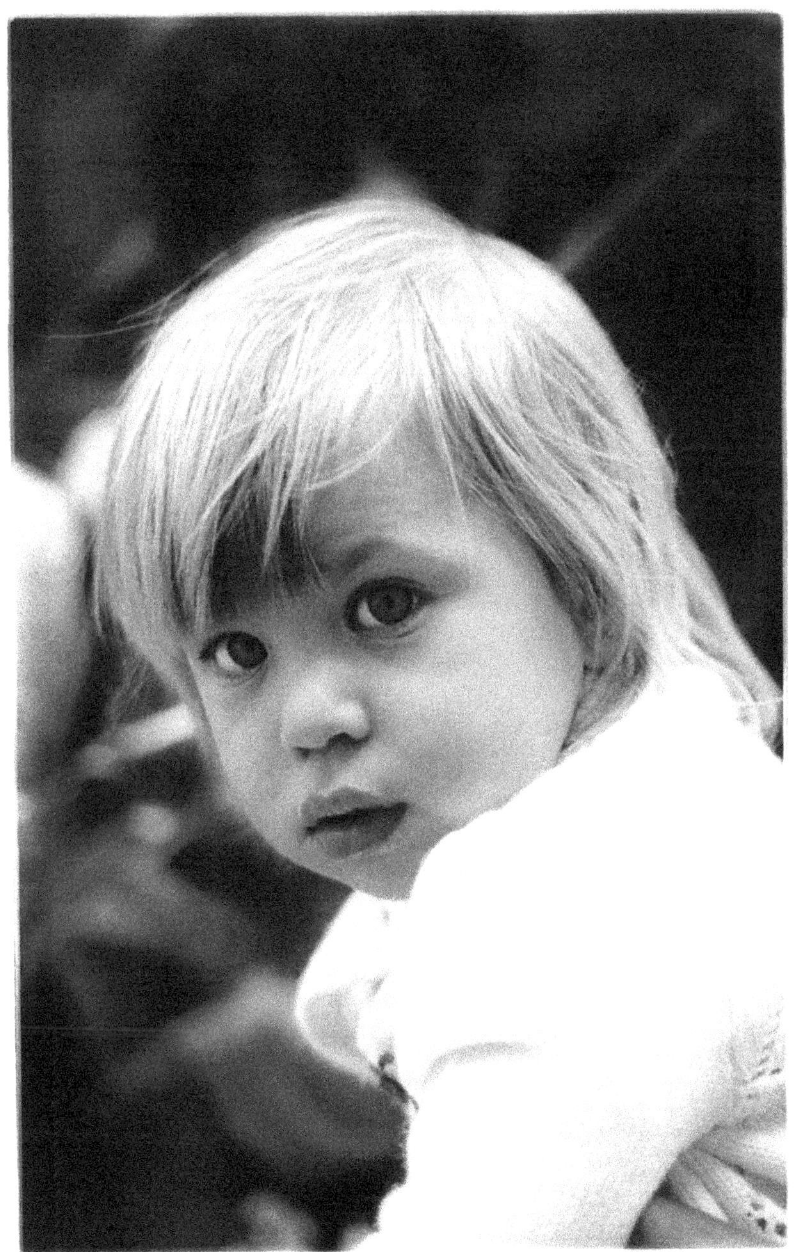

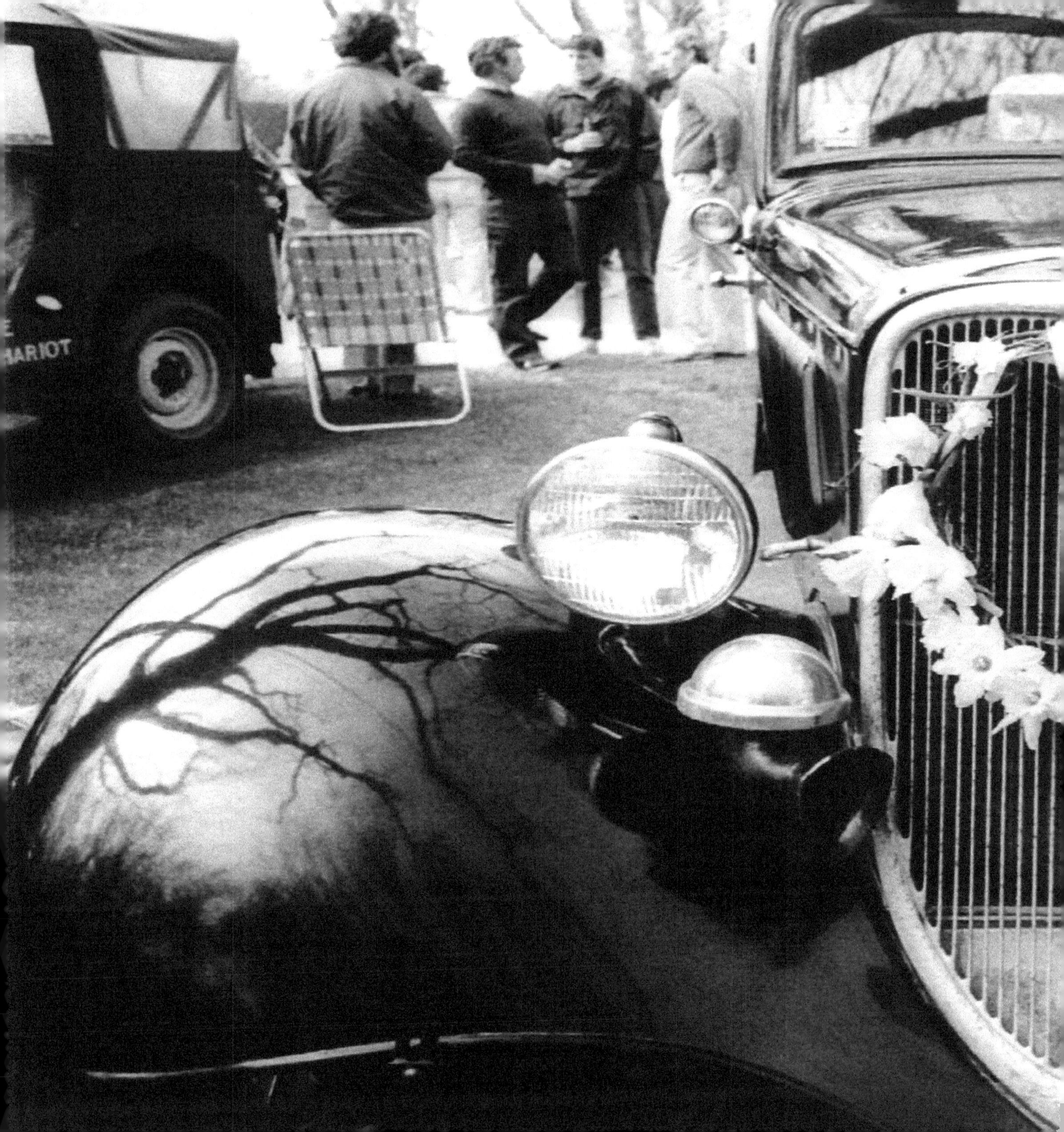

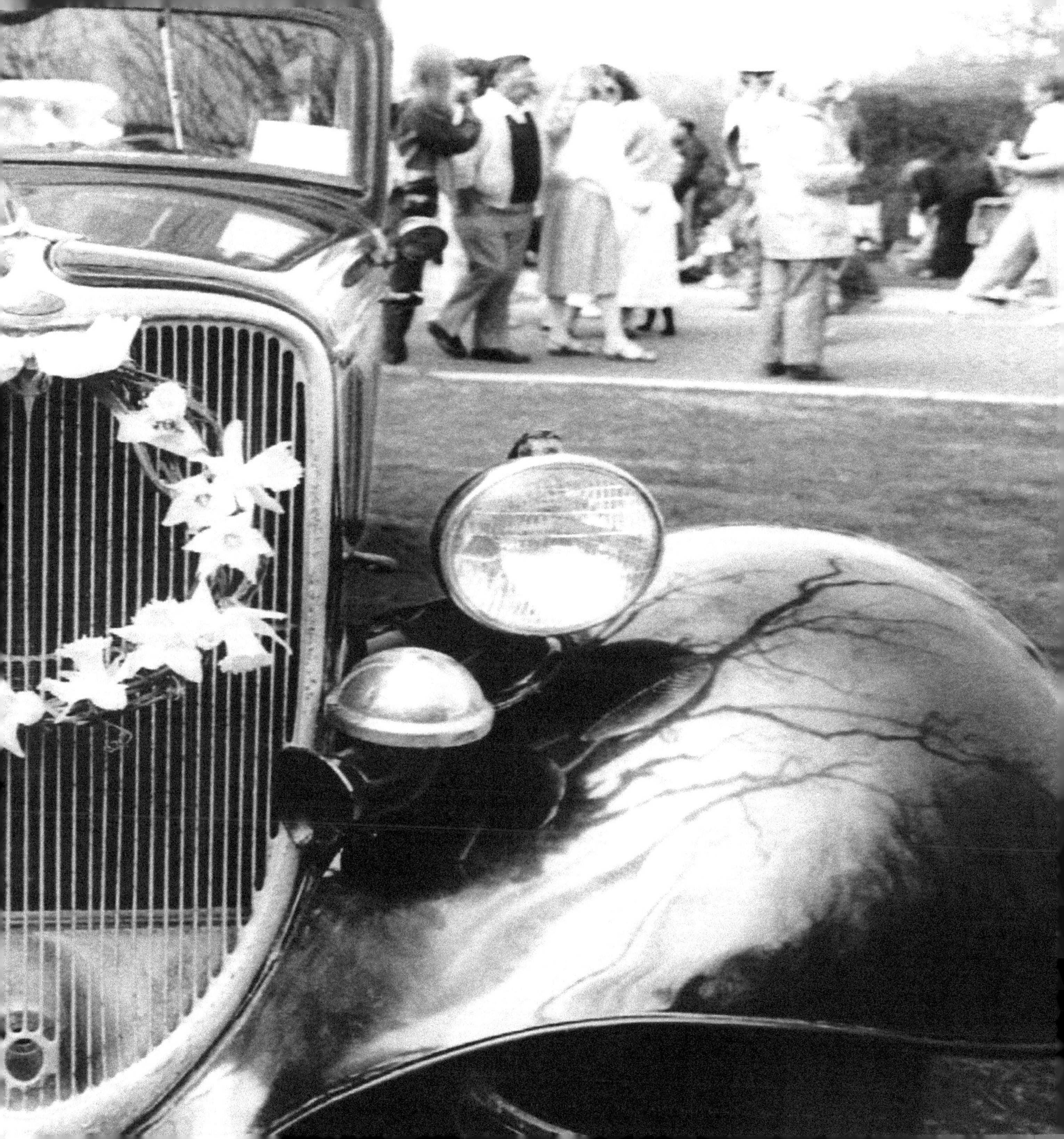

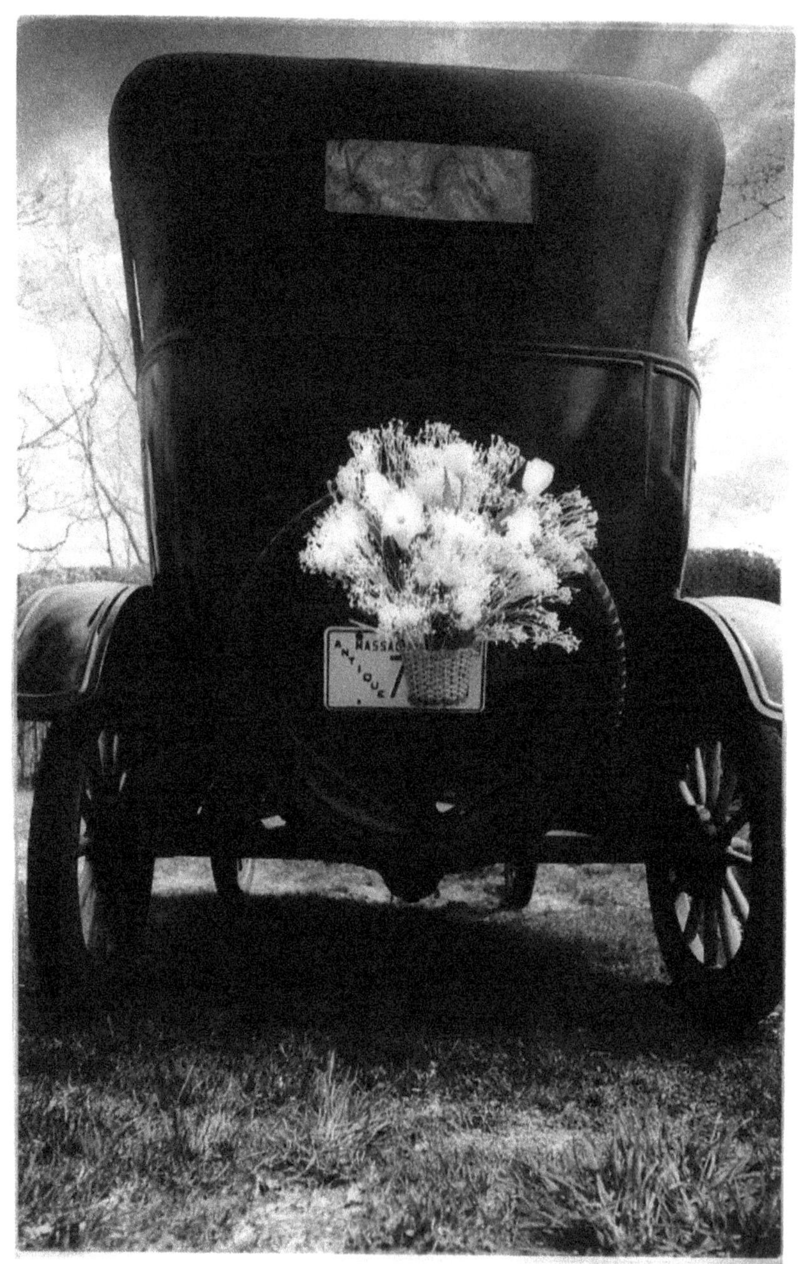
ANTIQUE

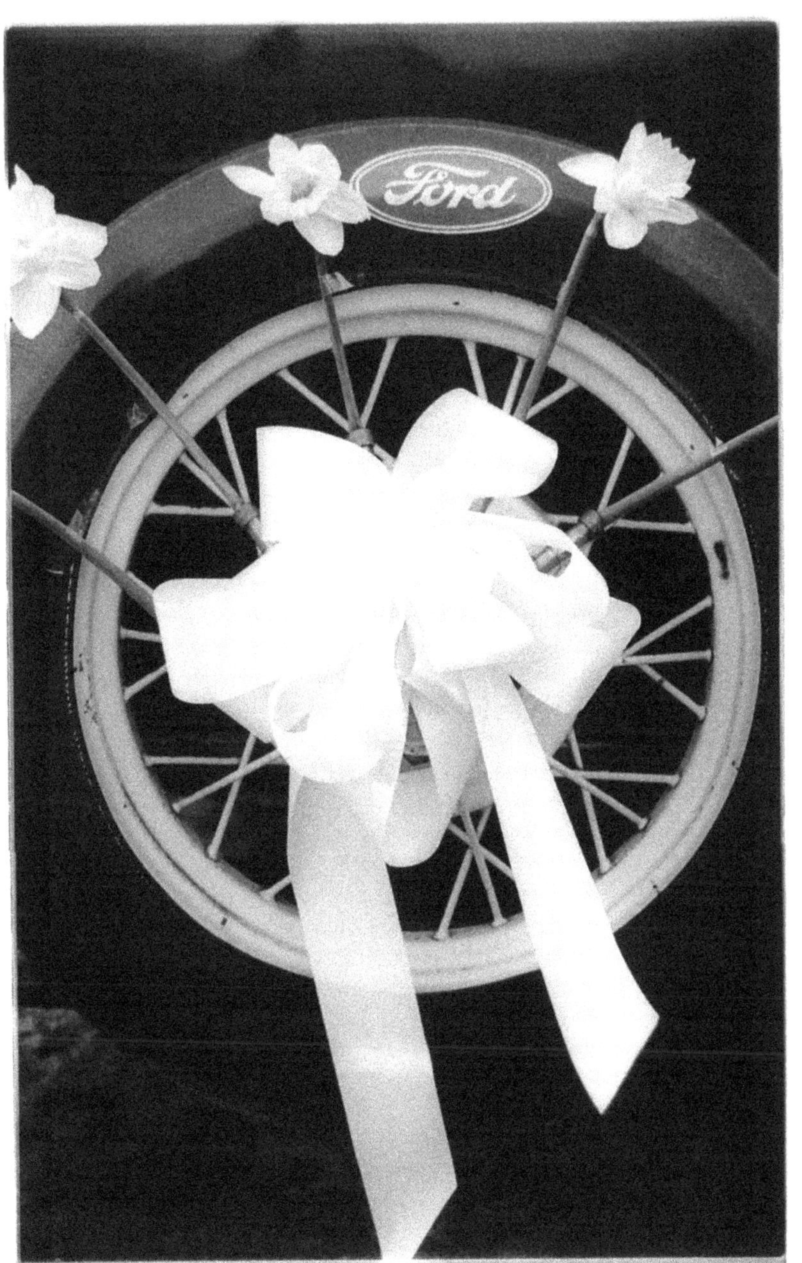
Ford

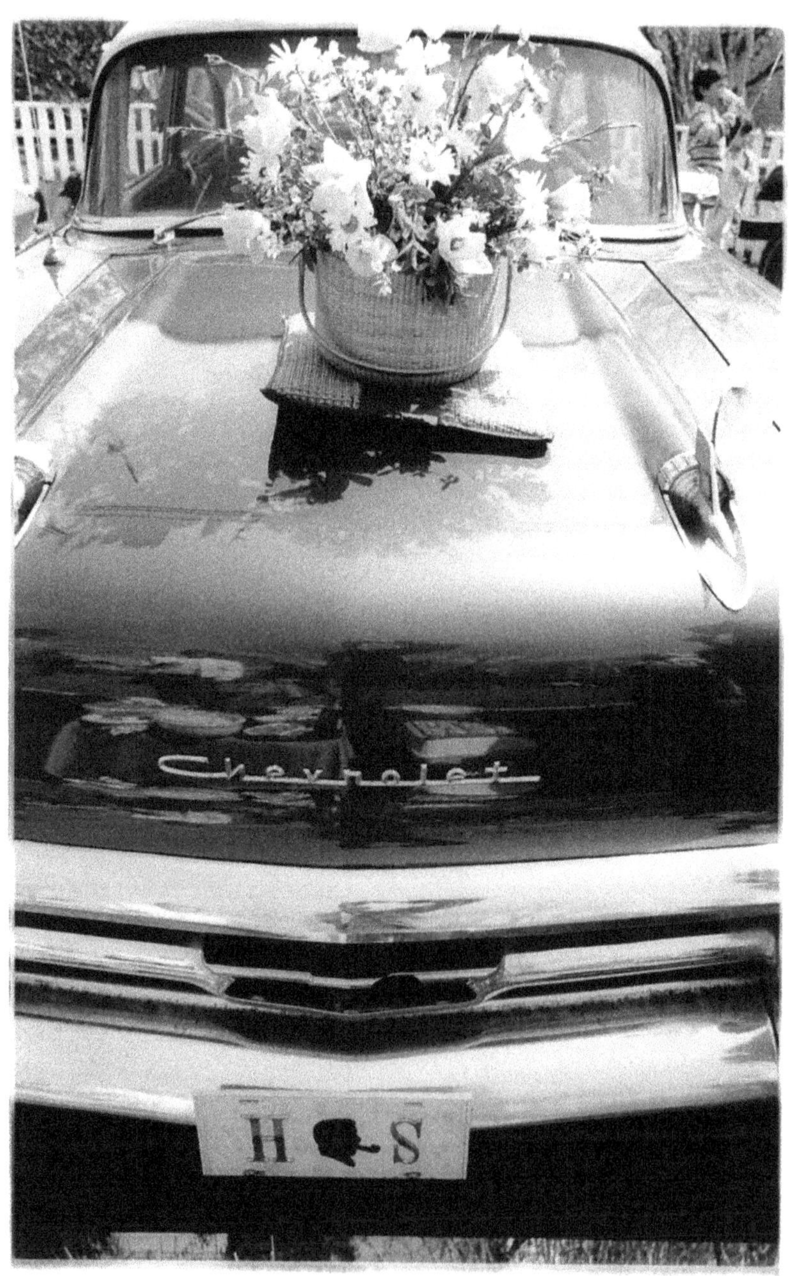
Chevrolet
H S

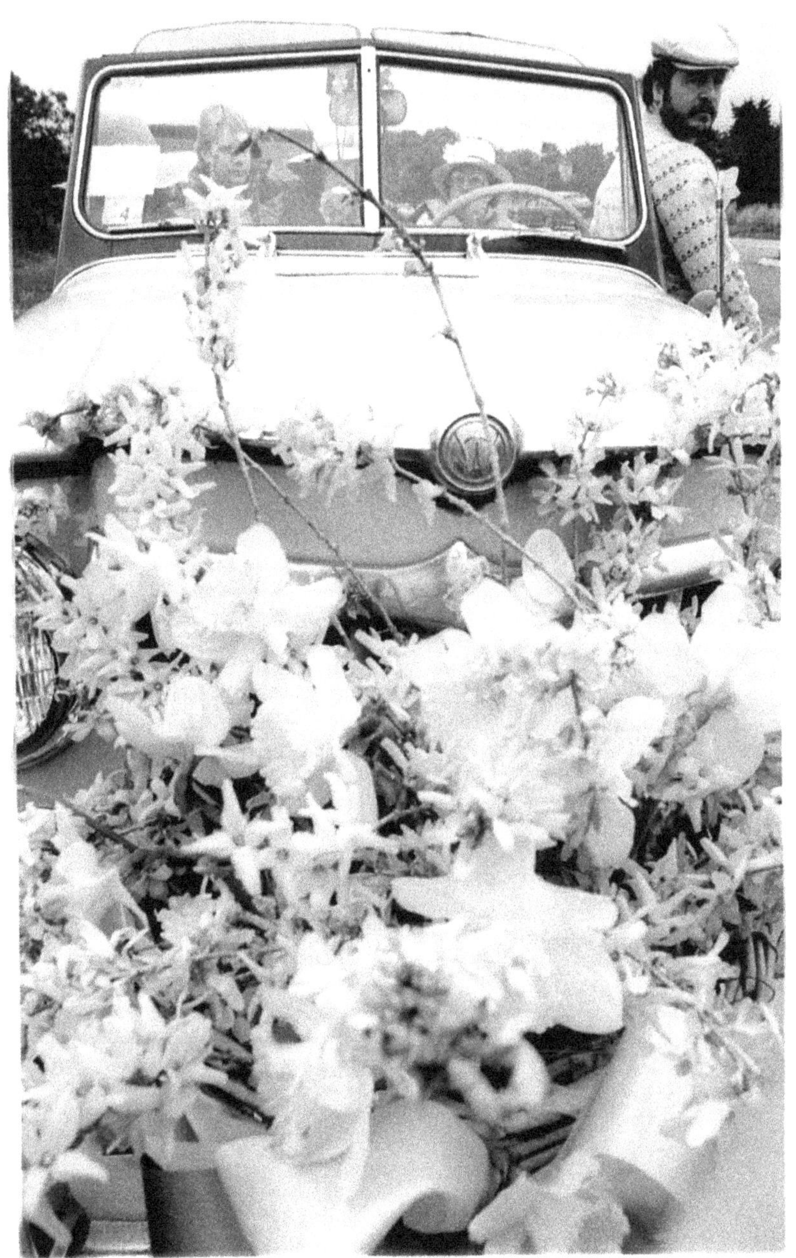

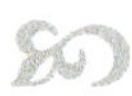

Nantucket Island
Saturday, April 1980
Early evening. Back in my room.
So tired I can hardly see straight.

Hitched a ride in a 1928 Ford Model A. Sat in the rumble seat. First time. Loved it! Feels like I had a dozen meals today, plus tasted a ton of desserts. If I had known what to expect I would never have had any breakfast at all.

Families were so gracious and willing to share and such pleasant company.

I couldn't say no when asked.

And didn't!

Good conversations, great company, beautiful people. What a fantastic day it was. I will sleep well tonight unless the gurgling in my stomach keeps me awake. I already can feel a rebellion brewing.

One thing I can say for sure, I won't be hungry for any dinner tonight. Maybe not even breakfast tomorrow . . .

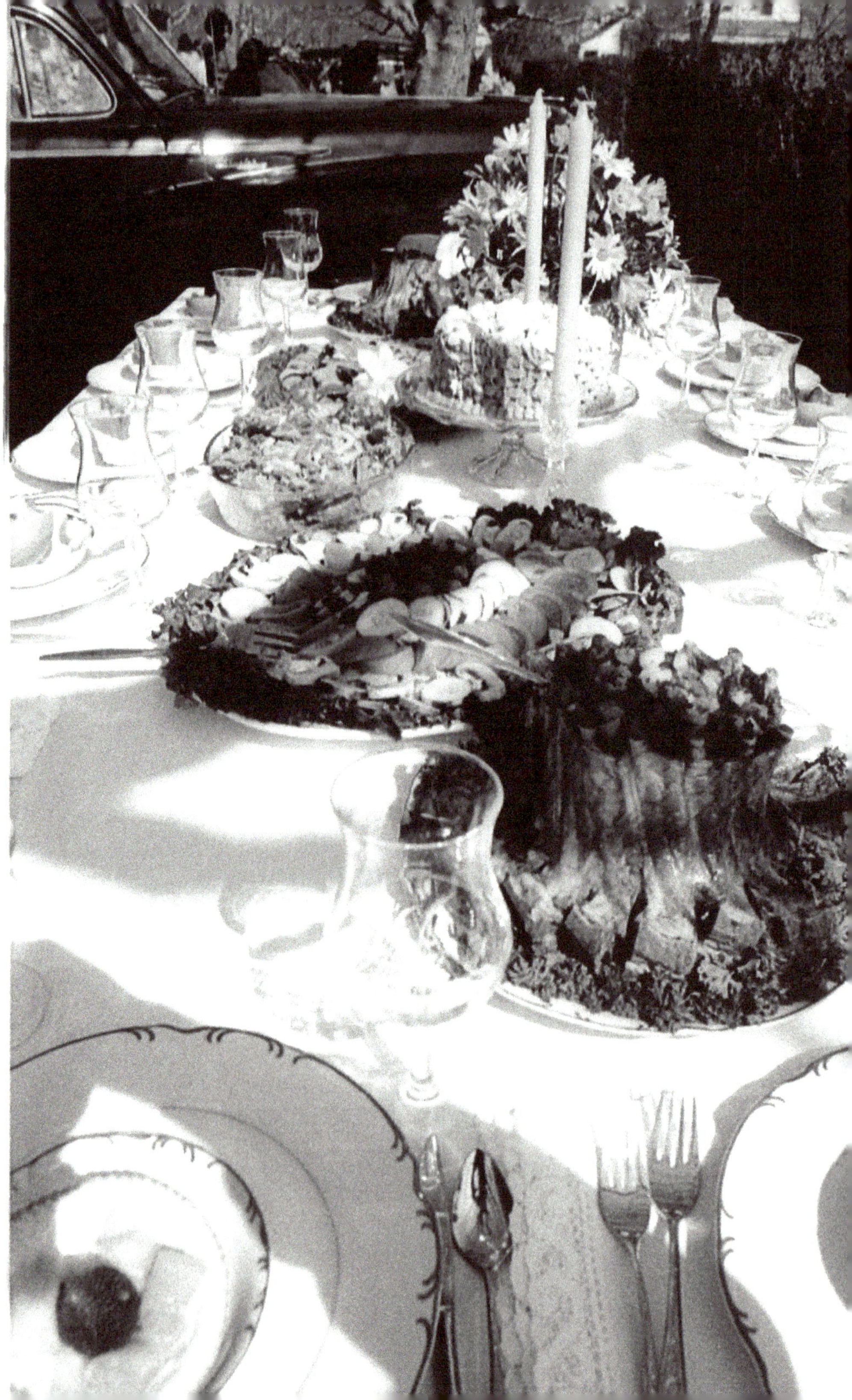

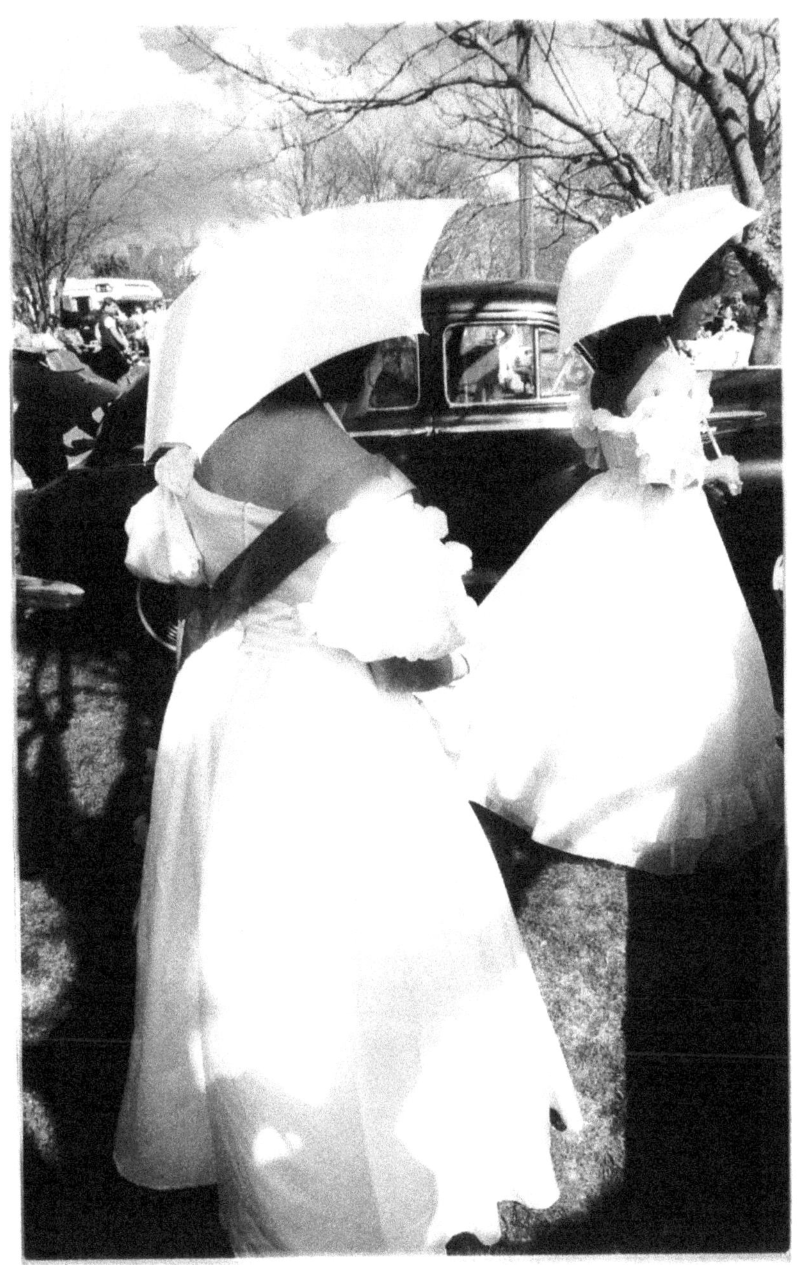

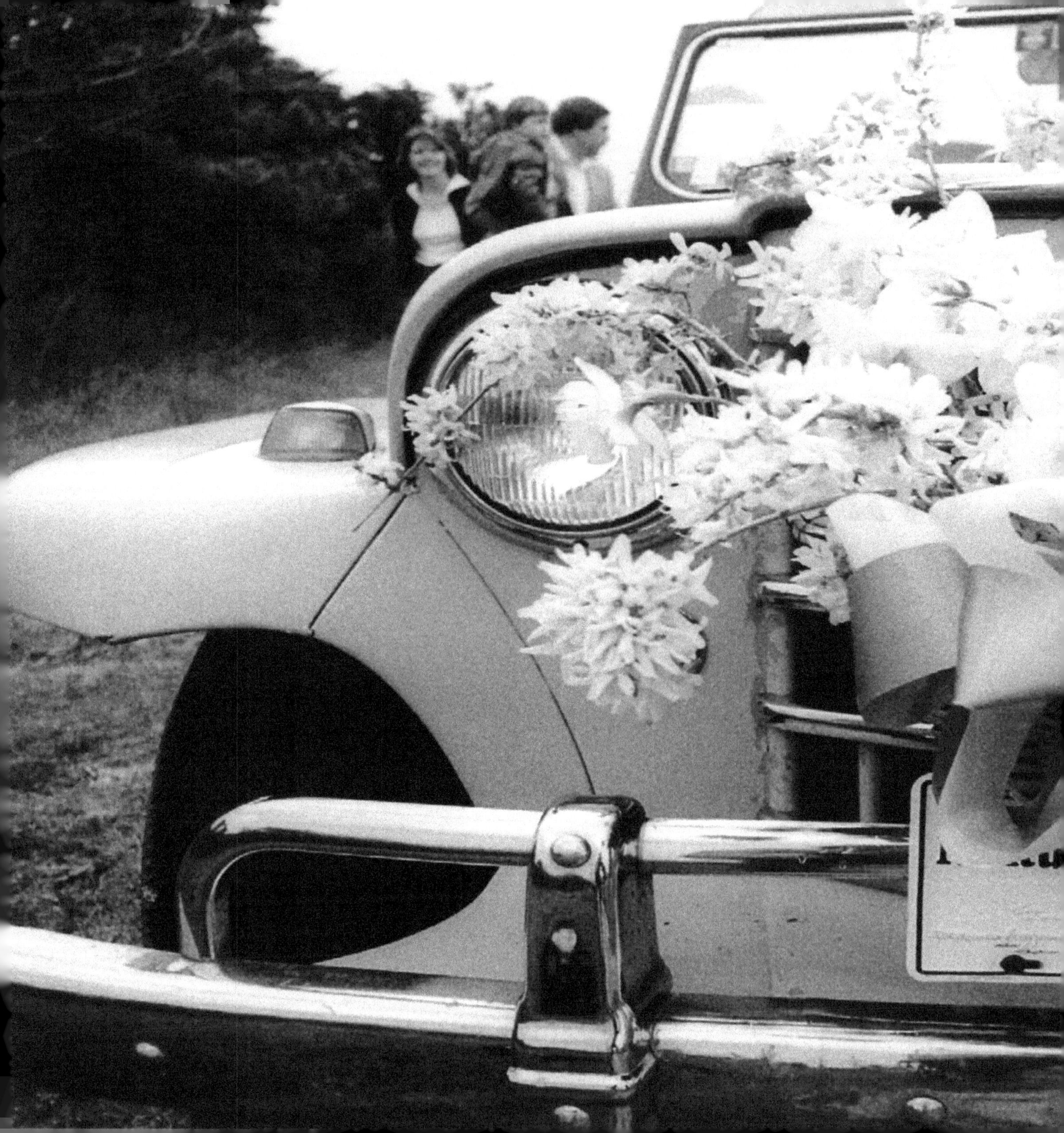

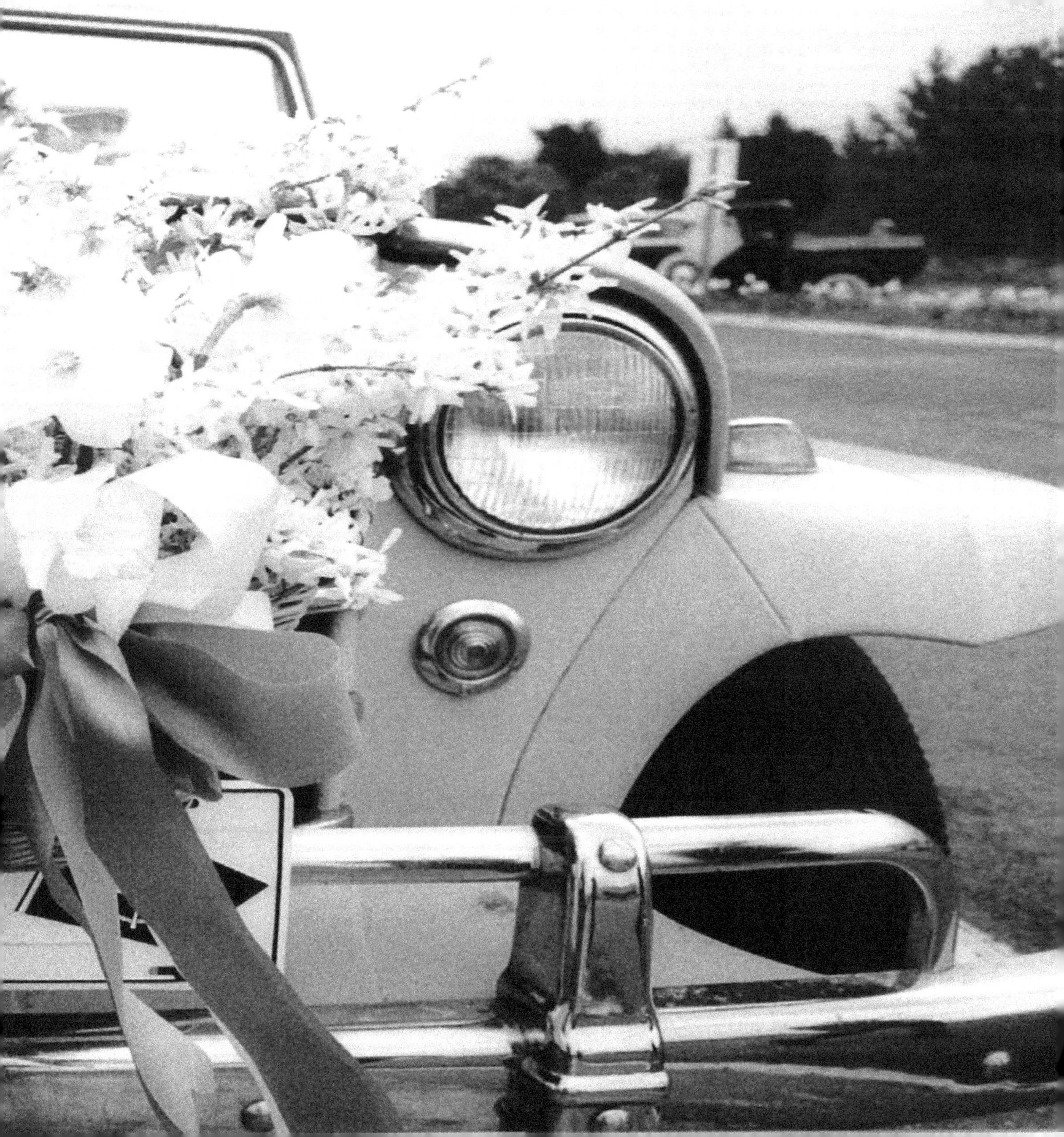

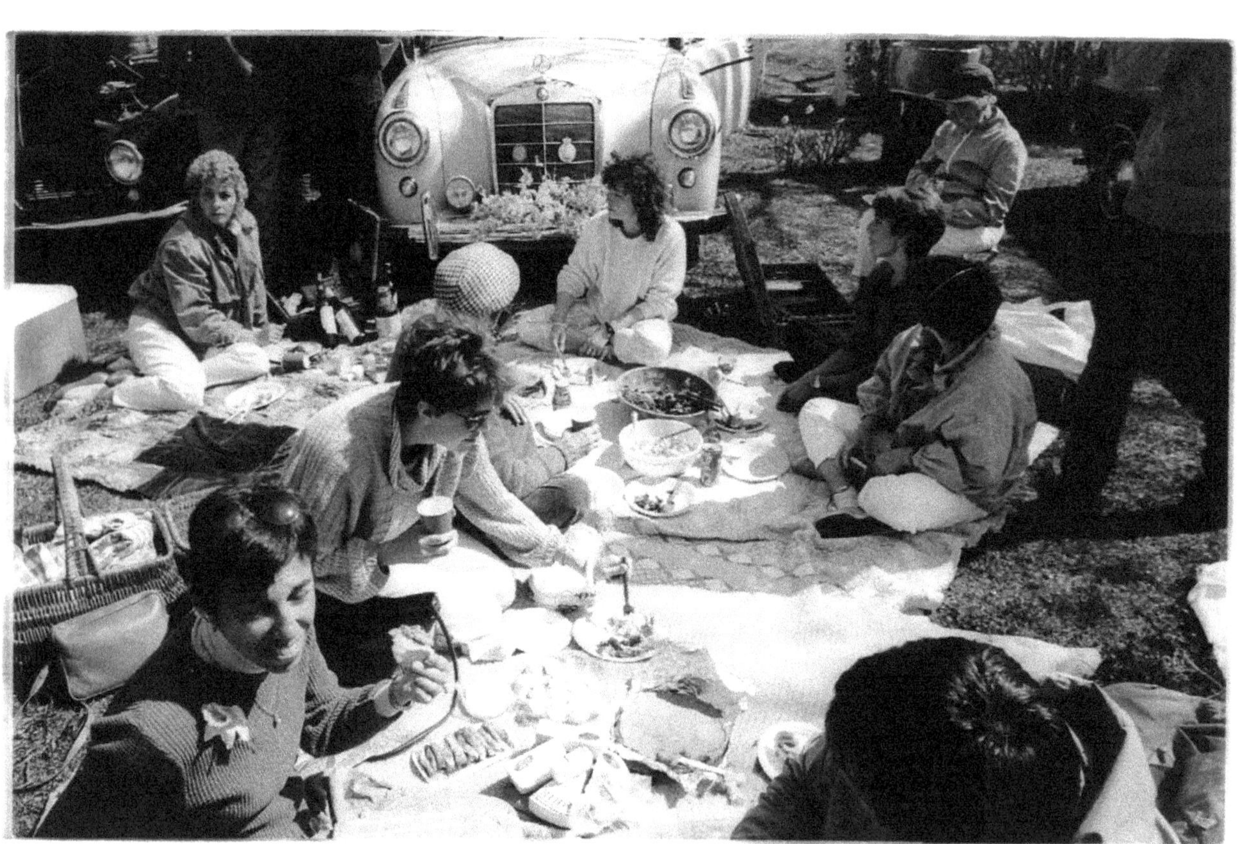

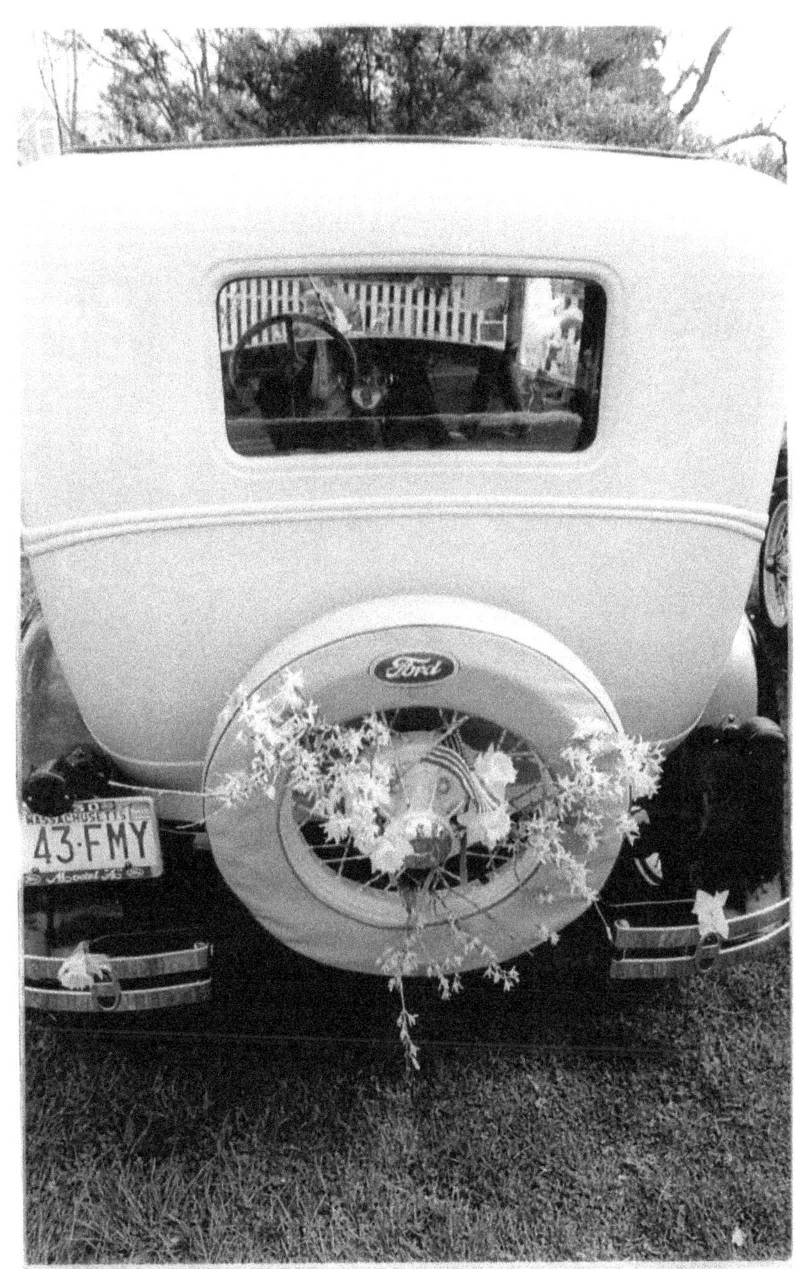
Ford
43·FMY

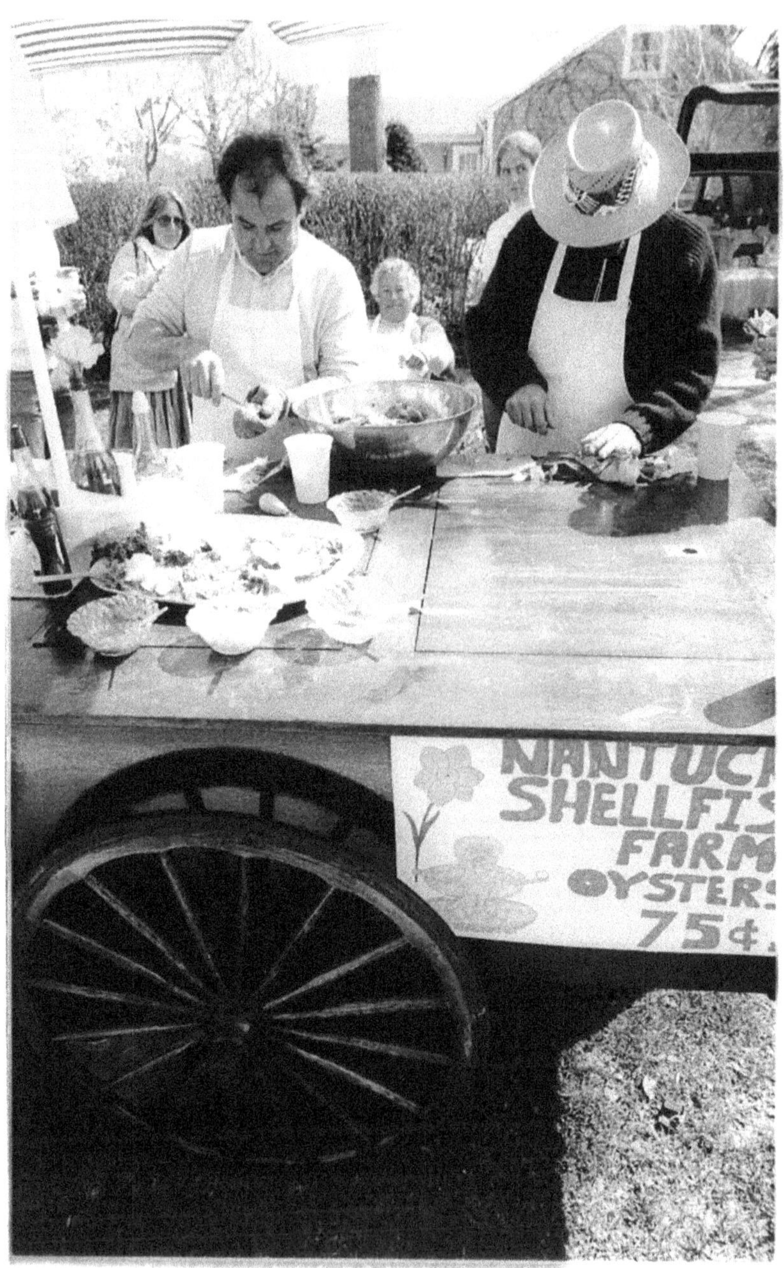
NANTUCK
SHELLFIS
FARM
OYSTERS
75¢.

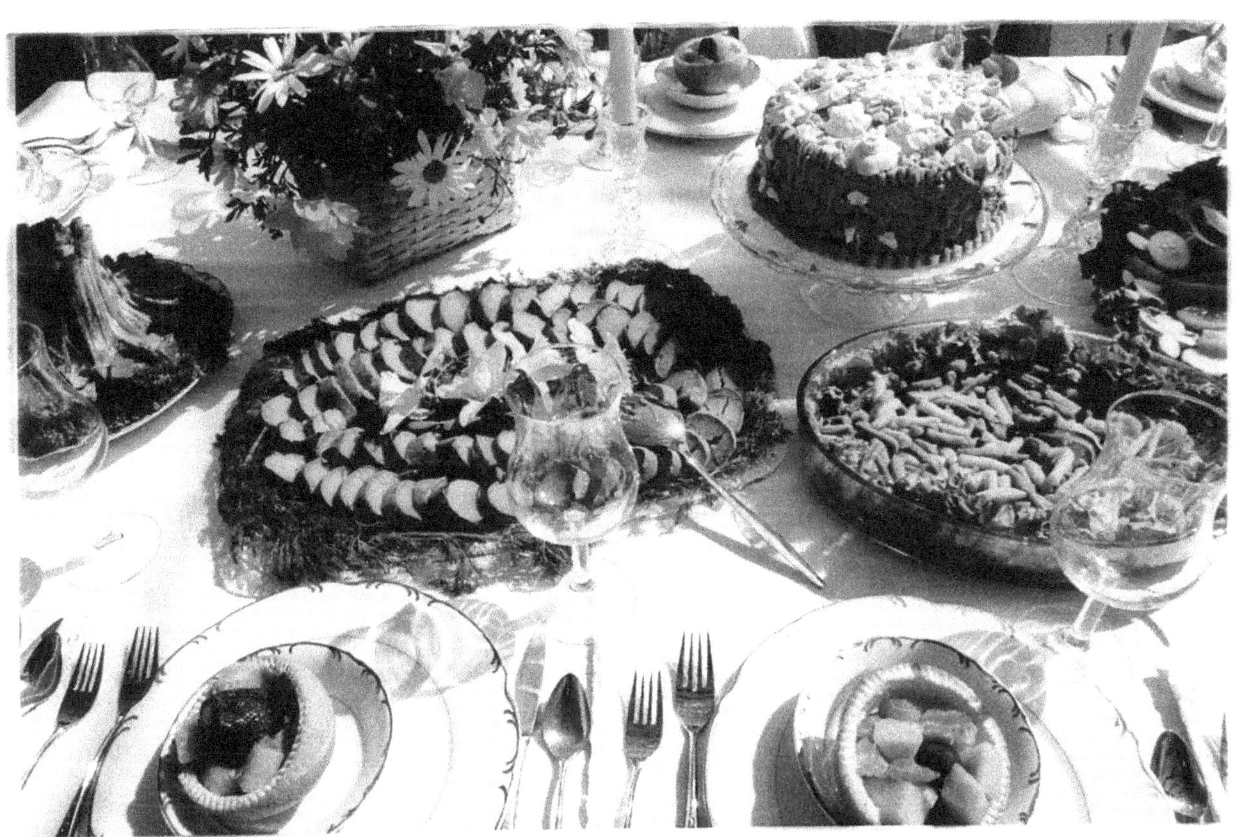

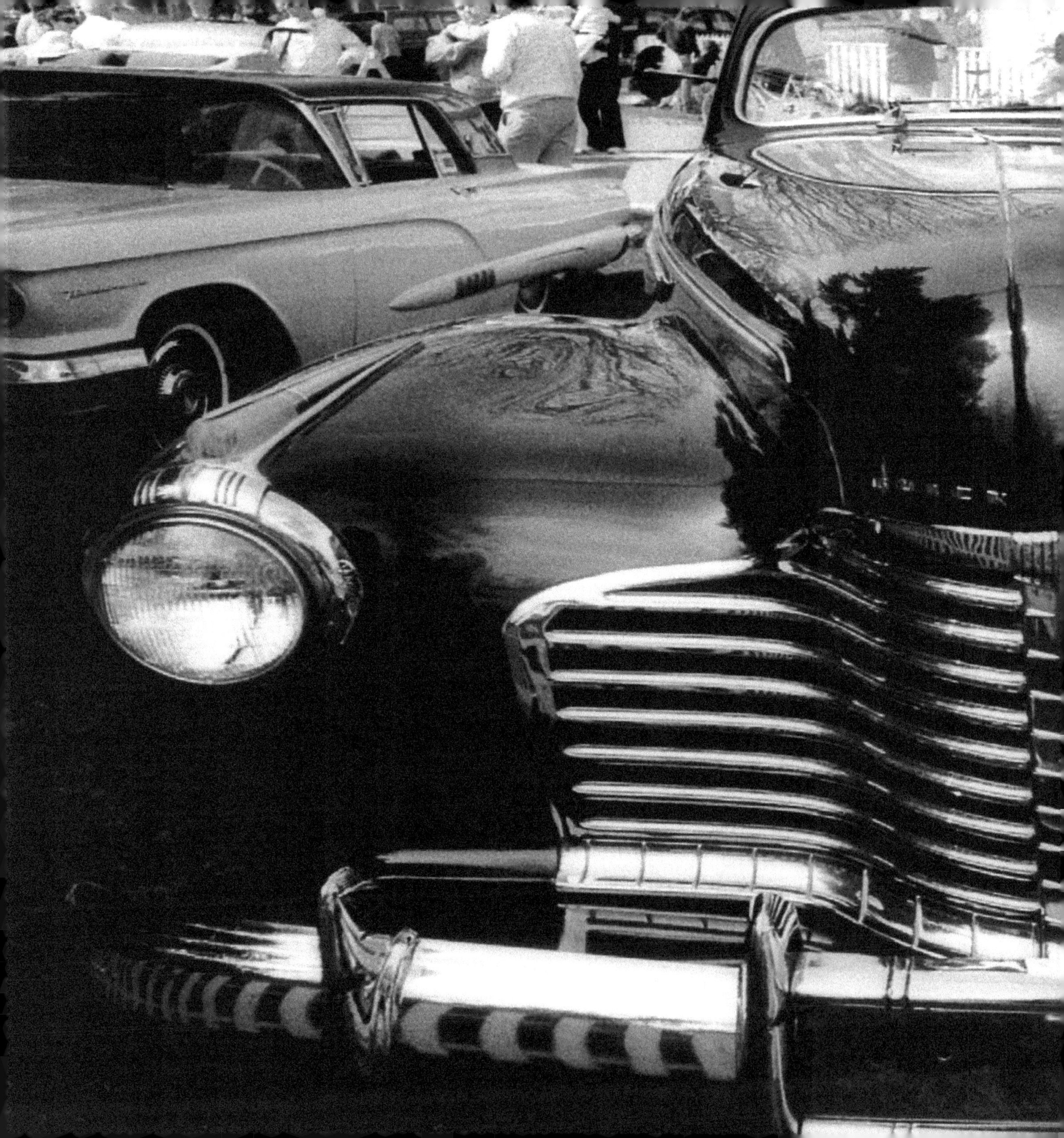

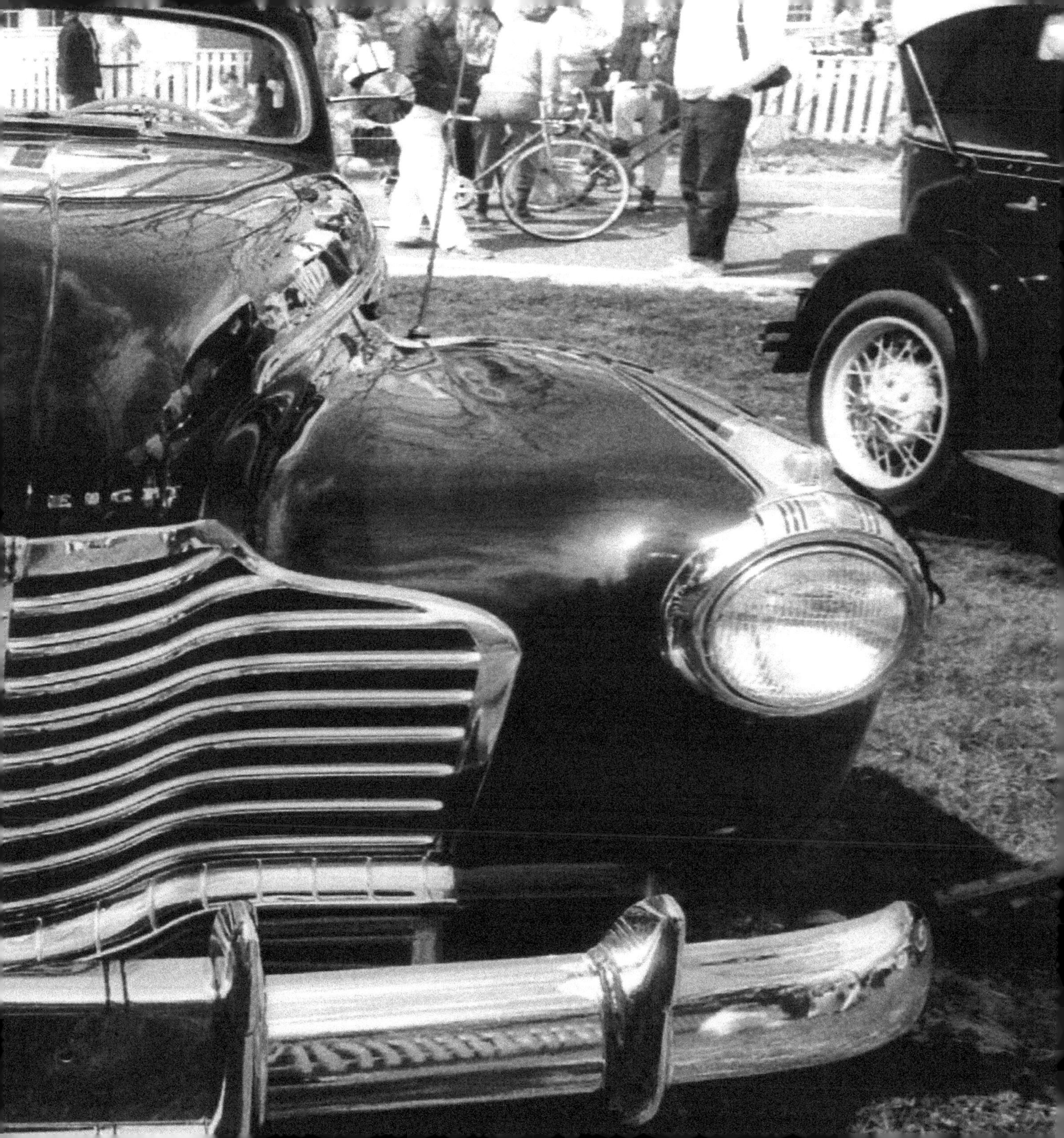

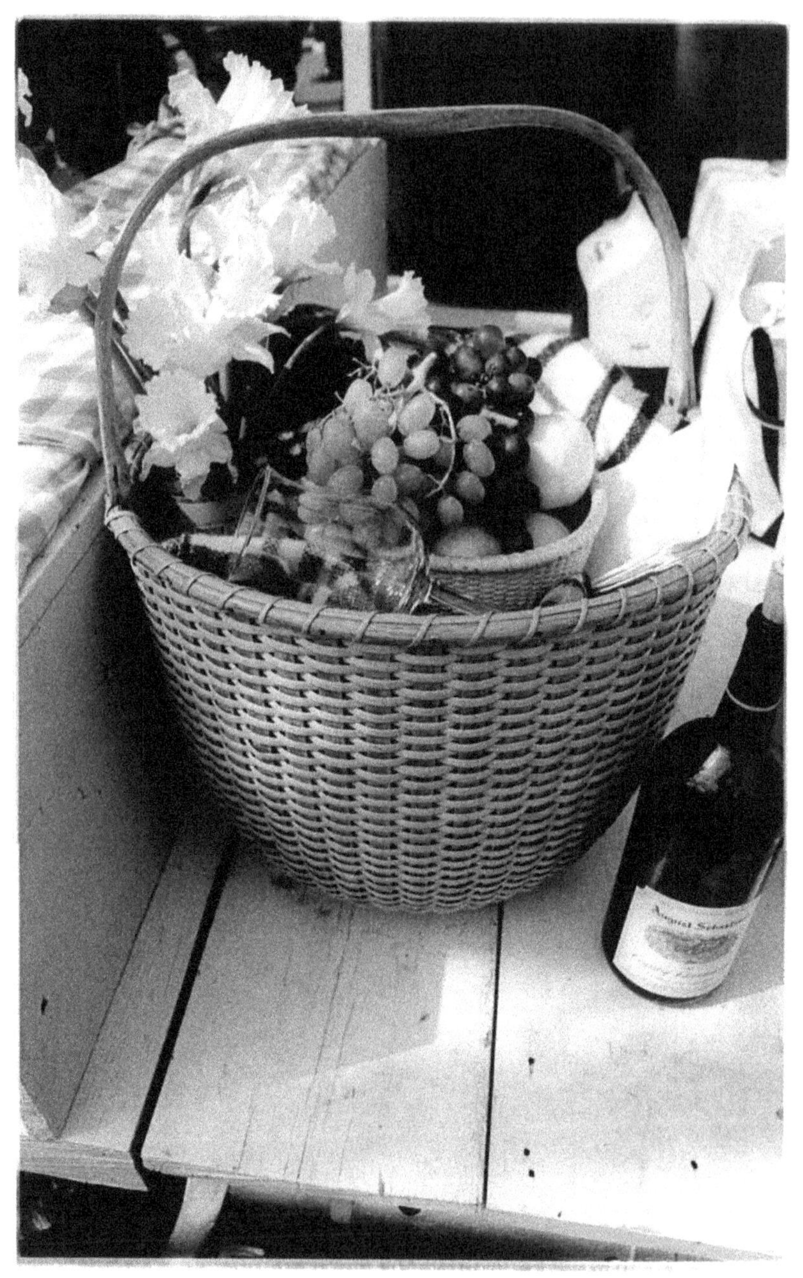

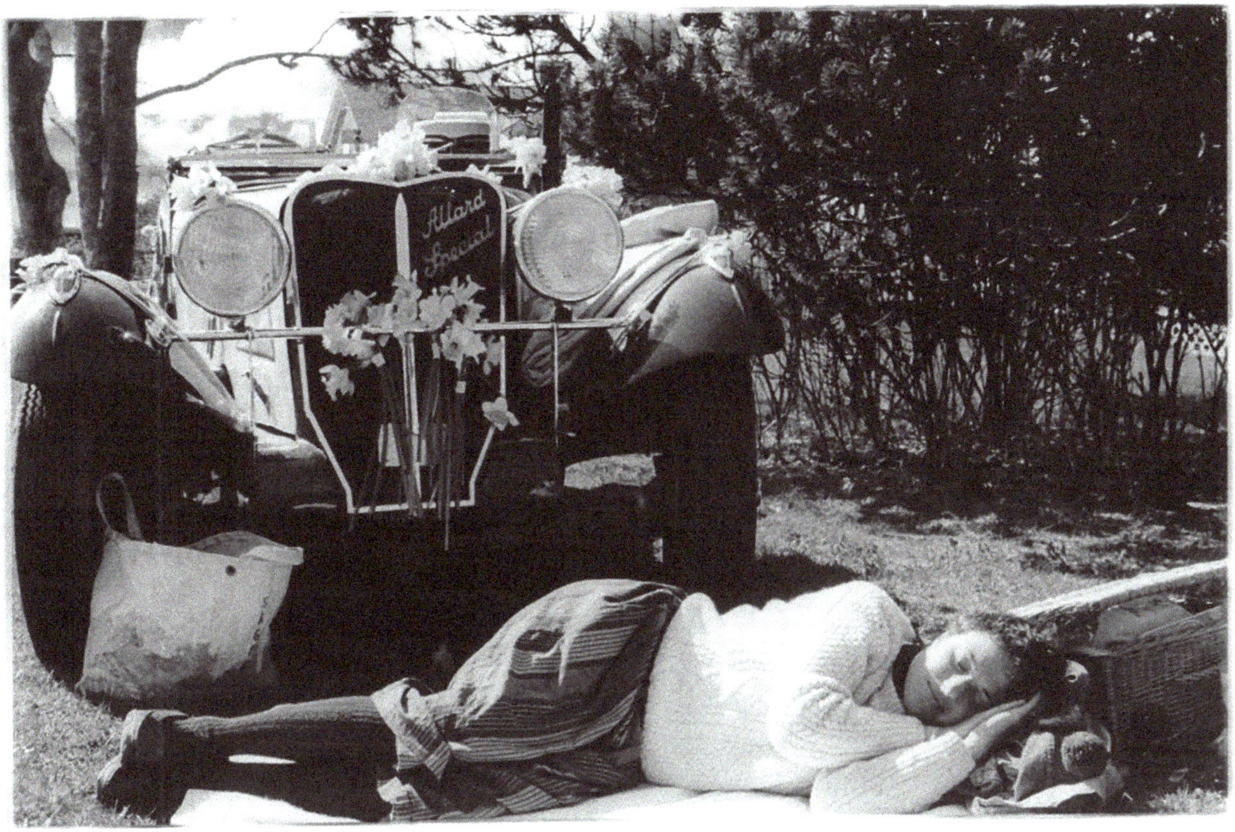

Nantucket Island
Saturday, April 1980
Late Afternoon.

To sleep . . . Perchance to dream . . .
To wish . . . To hope . . . Oh, to dream . . .

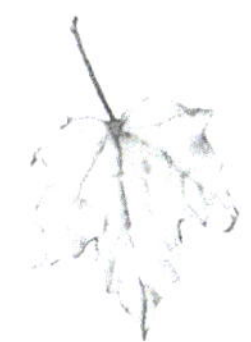

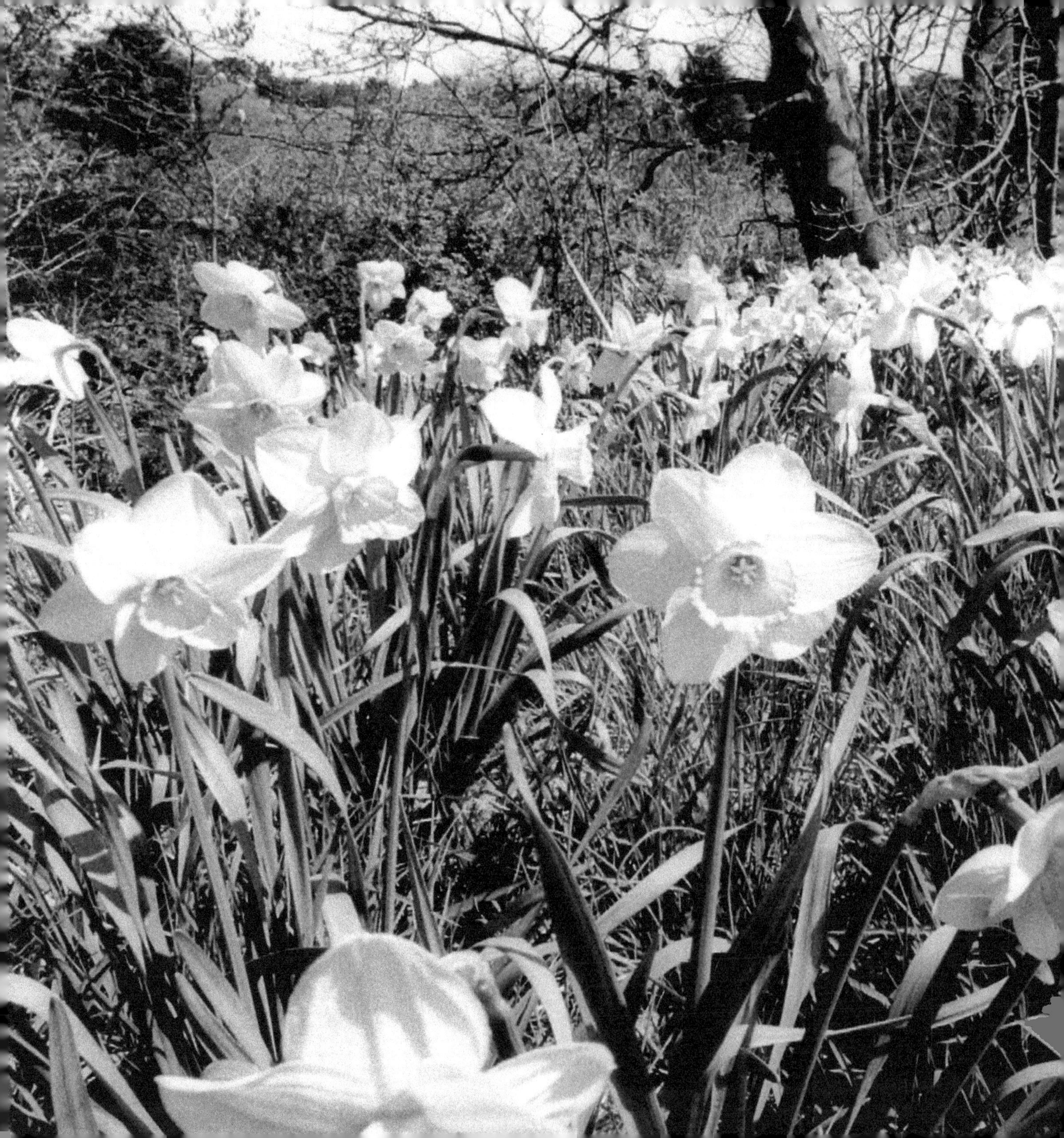

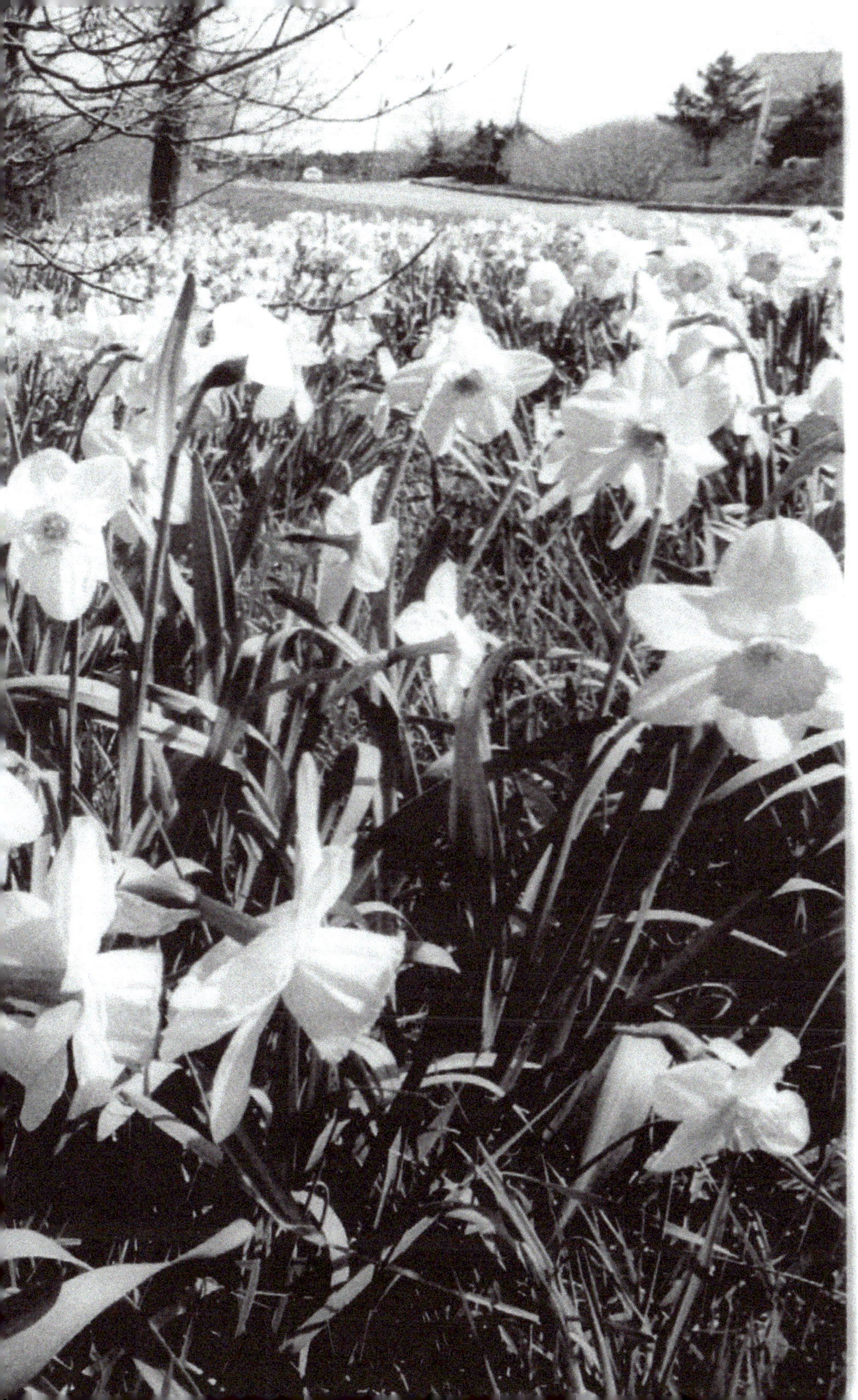

Siasconset
Sunday, April 1980
It's midnight. Can't sleep.

I have changed since I left my hometown. I've shifted slightly for some time, and even now, I still stand a little off balance.

Springtime will forever be a season of reflections for me, like ripples in a pond edging outward. It is a season that will remind me of when I lost my one true love, Martha.

If only I could be the master of time and space and return before that fateful day and whisk her away to safety. What dreams I have of us together if the shape of things had played differently.

I have quickly fallen for Nantucket. Living here, meeting good people, and watching the changing seasons has made me feel better about my life, and yet, a spring as unique and different as this one makes me realize even more how much I miss my Martha.

Glorious days as I've witnessed here on this island, like today, are meant to be shared with the ones we love.

I adore springtime, the trees and plants stirring into bloom, their floral scents pushed by the breeze, and the rich, fecund smell of the earth as plants occupy themselves with the task of growing.

I am touched the most when the flowering trees find their voices and scatter their songs along the roadside with such vibrant shades of pinks and white.

It never fails to amaze me how vivid the reds and pinks shine so boldly and how lace-like the dogwoods look as if laden with snow, a gentle reminder of the circle of life.

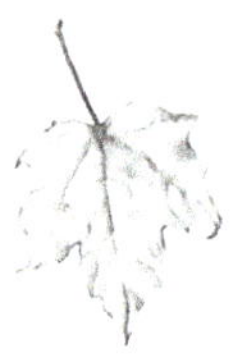

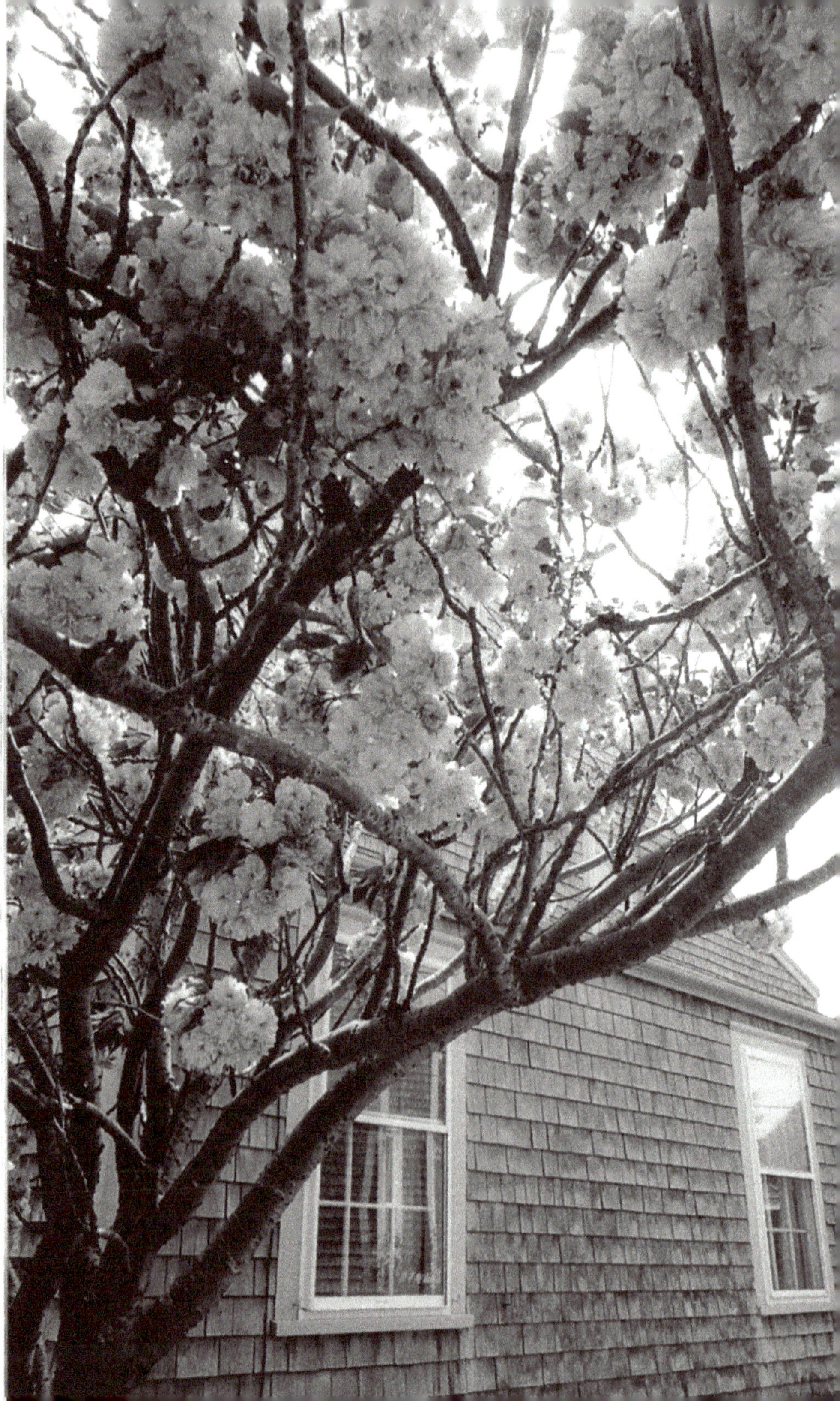

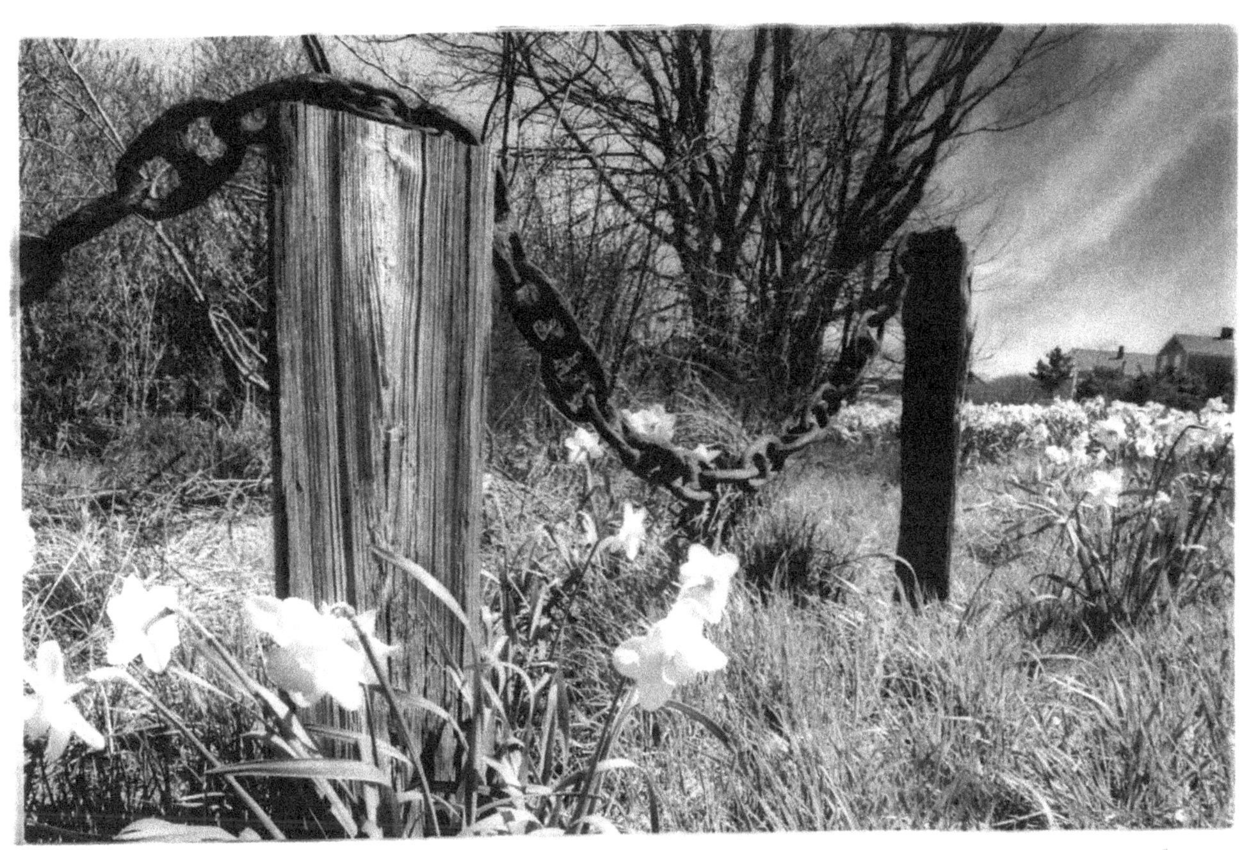

Polpis Road

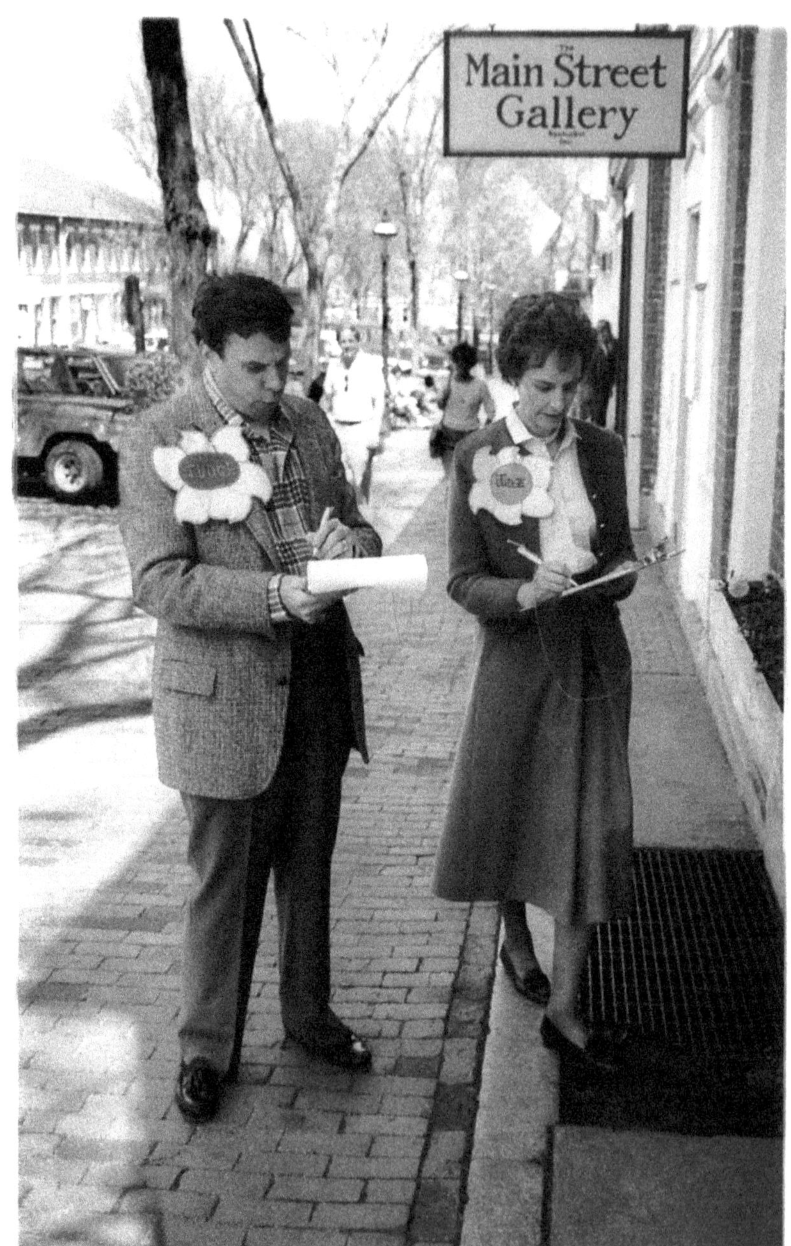

Judging Window Displays

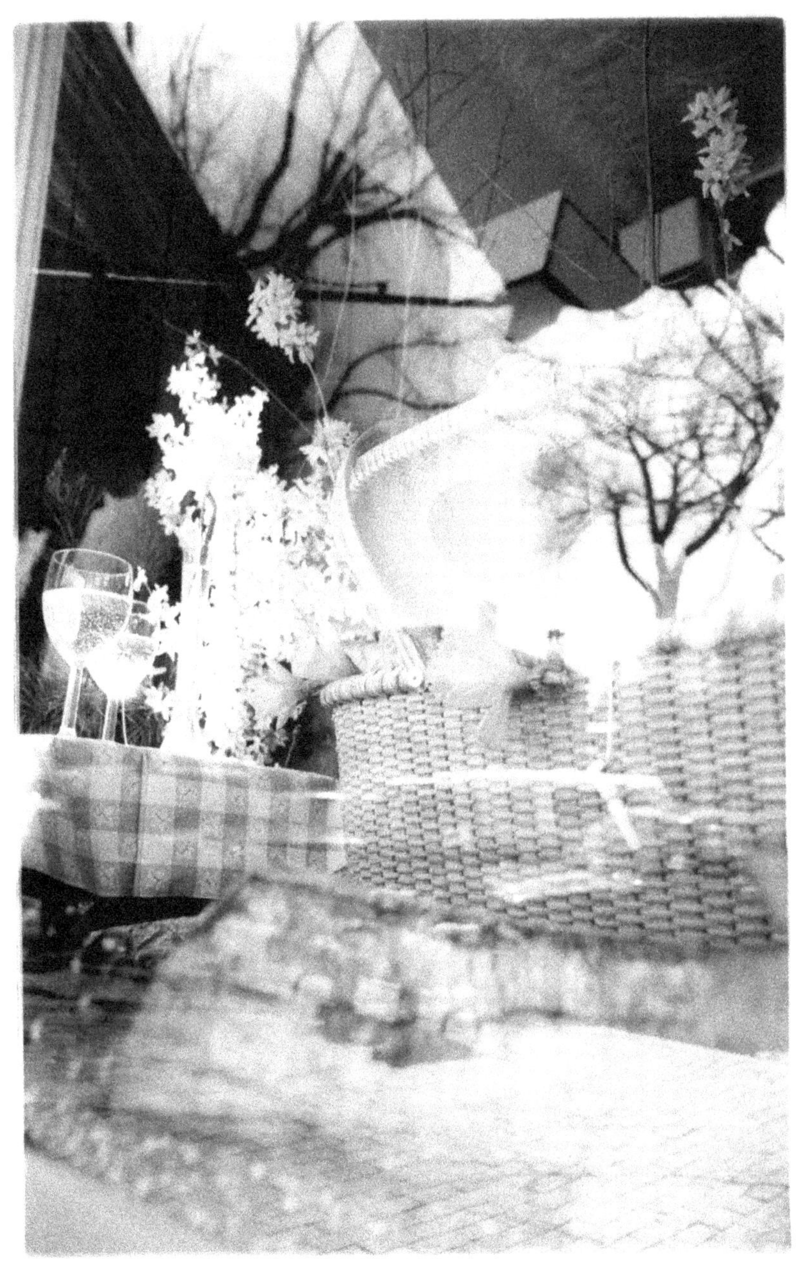

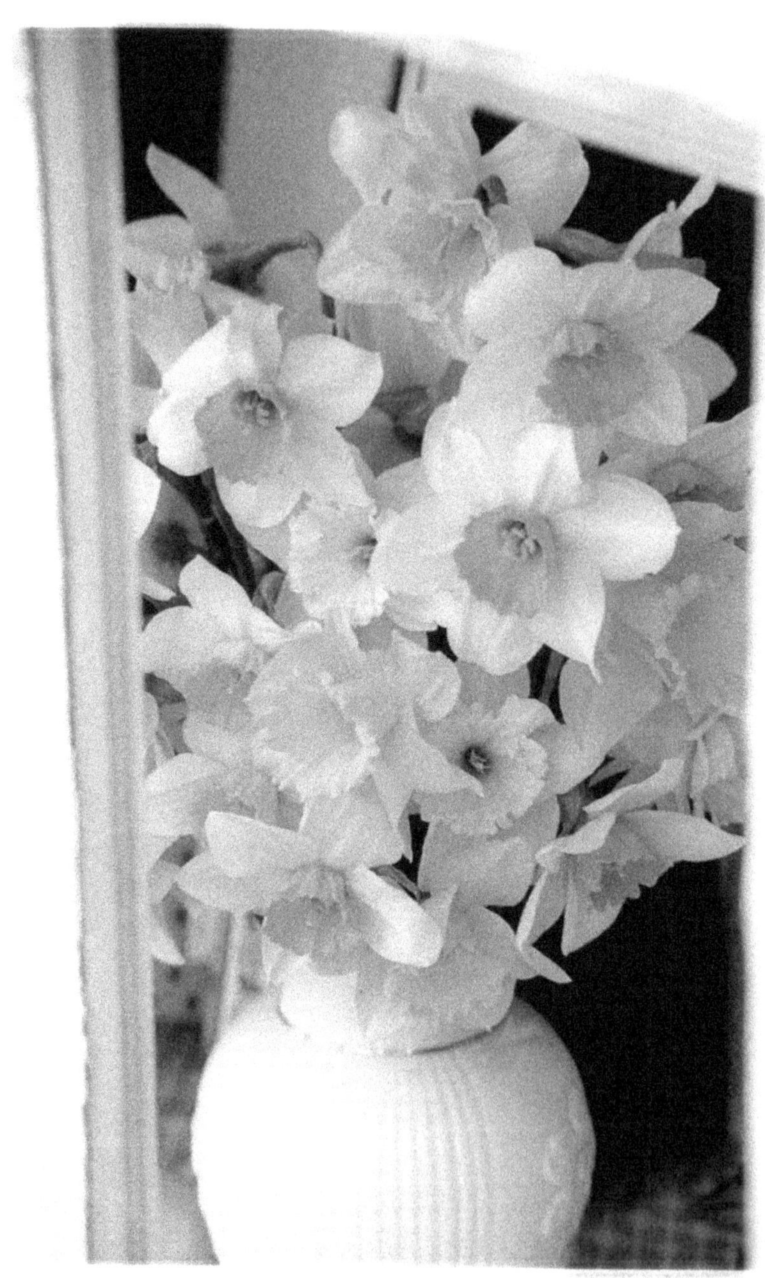

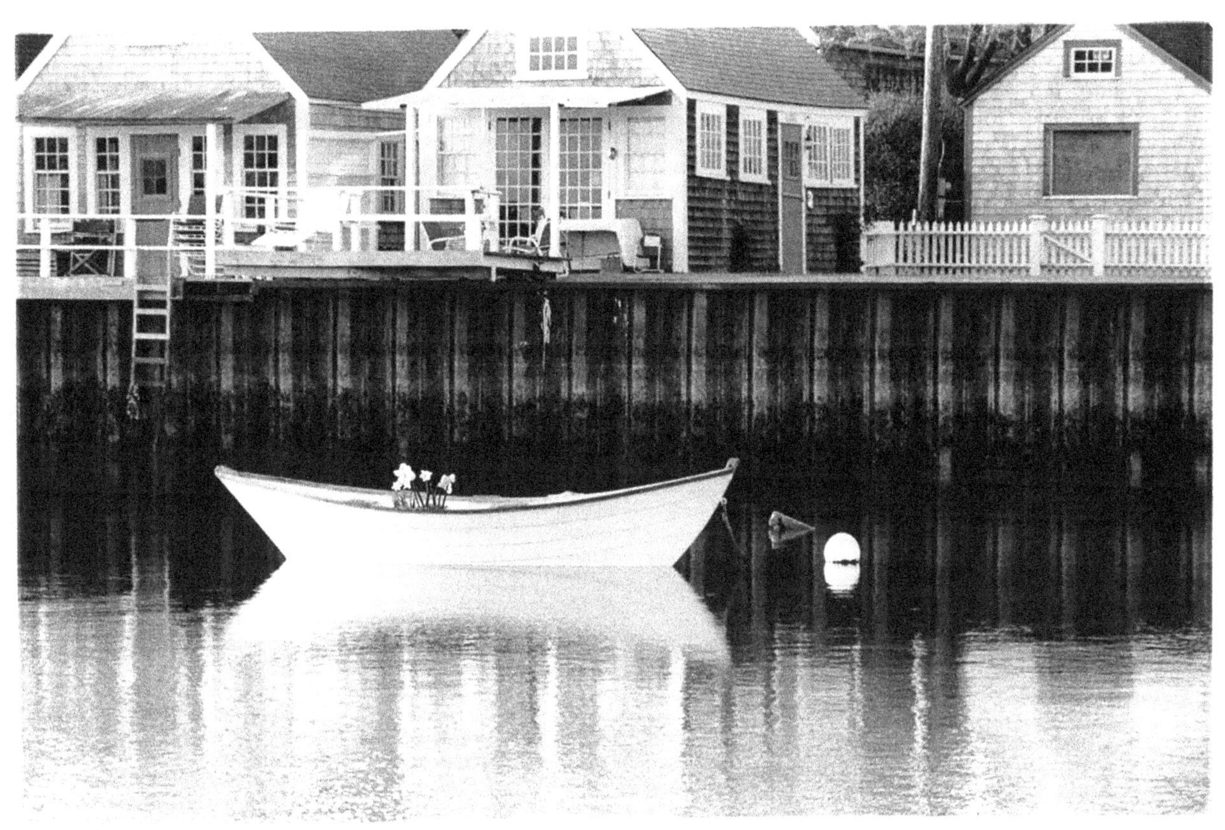

On The Wharf

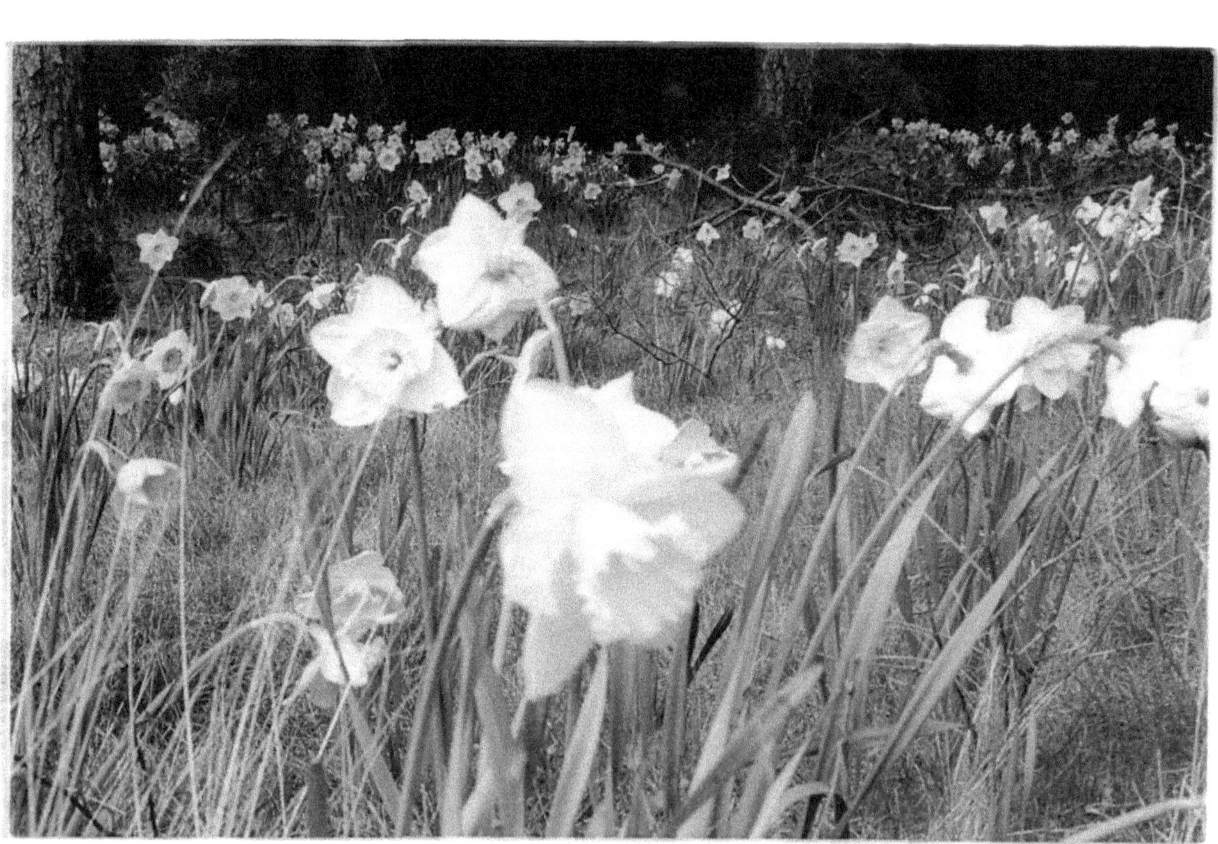

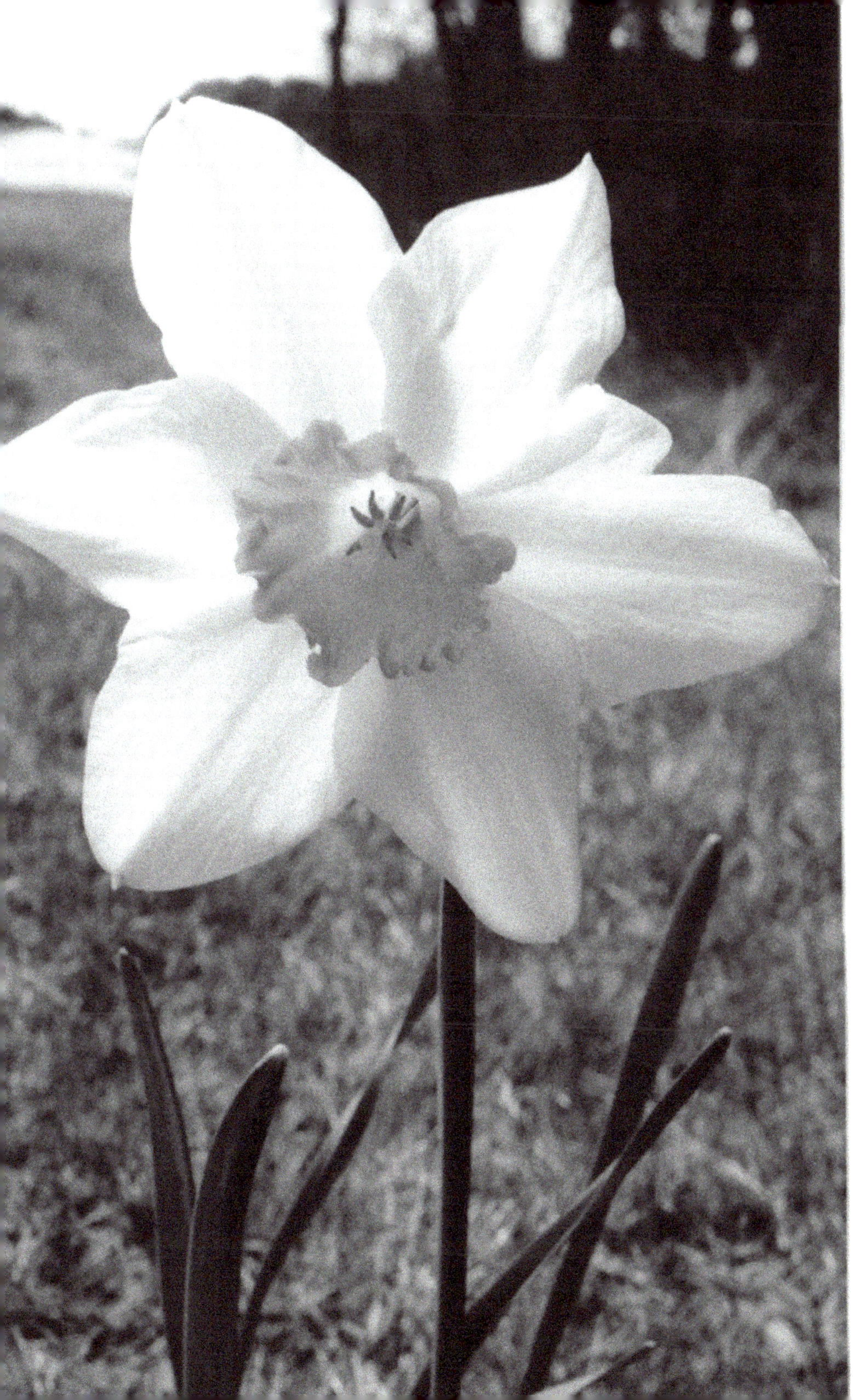

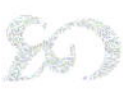

We all have to make our dreams for ourselves and make the most concerted, most robust and forthright effort to follow our dreams and sustain them–protect them–so they bloom and enrich our lives.

They don't just appear out of thin air, and it is the saddest loss for everyone when we let doubt and fear control our thoughts and steal our dreams.

Most of us spend more energy devoted to denying that fear can take control over us than we do to confront it. Nothing is easy, especially following a dream. There will always be hills and valleys. As long as we can pick ourselves up, ignore the grass stains, and continue reaching for the light, we'll have no regrets.

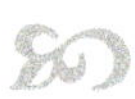

Sunday, April 1980.

I had a pleasant experience today. While photographing the Garden Club Daffodil Flower Show, I met Jean MacAusland, publisher of Gourmet Magazine. She is the reason the Nantucket Garden Club invited The American Daffodil Society to sponsor the Daffodil festival.

Mrs. MacAusland and I sat down for tea after she finished judging the flower show. We had a delightful chat, and she told me in 1974 the Garden Club set a goal to plant more than a million daffodil bulbs, and have just ordered over eight tons of bulbs to be shipped directly from the Netherlands.

She was pleased to hear how much I enjoyed the classic car parade. It was an idea she and her friend H. Flint Ranney started two years ago. I told her I thought it was something they should never stop doing. Who doesn't like a classic car, a picnic, and daffodils?

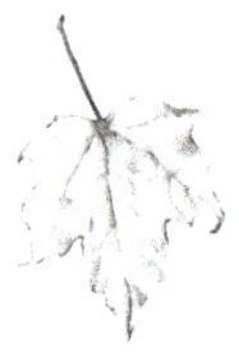

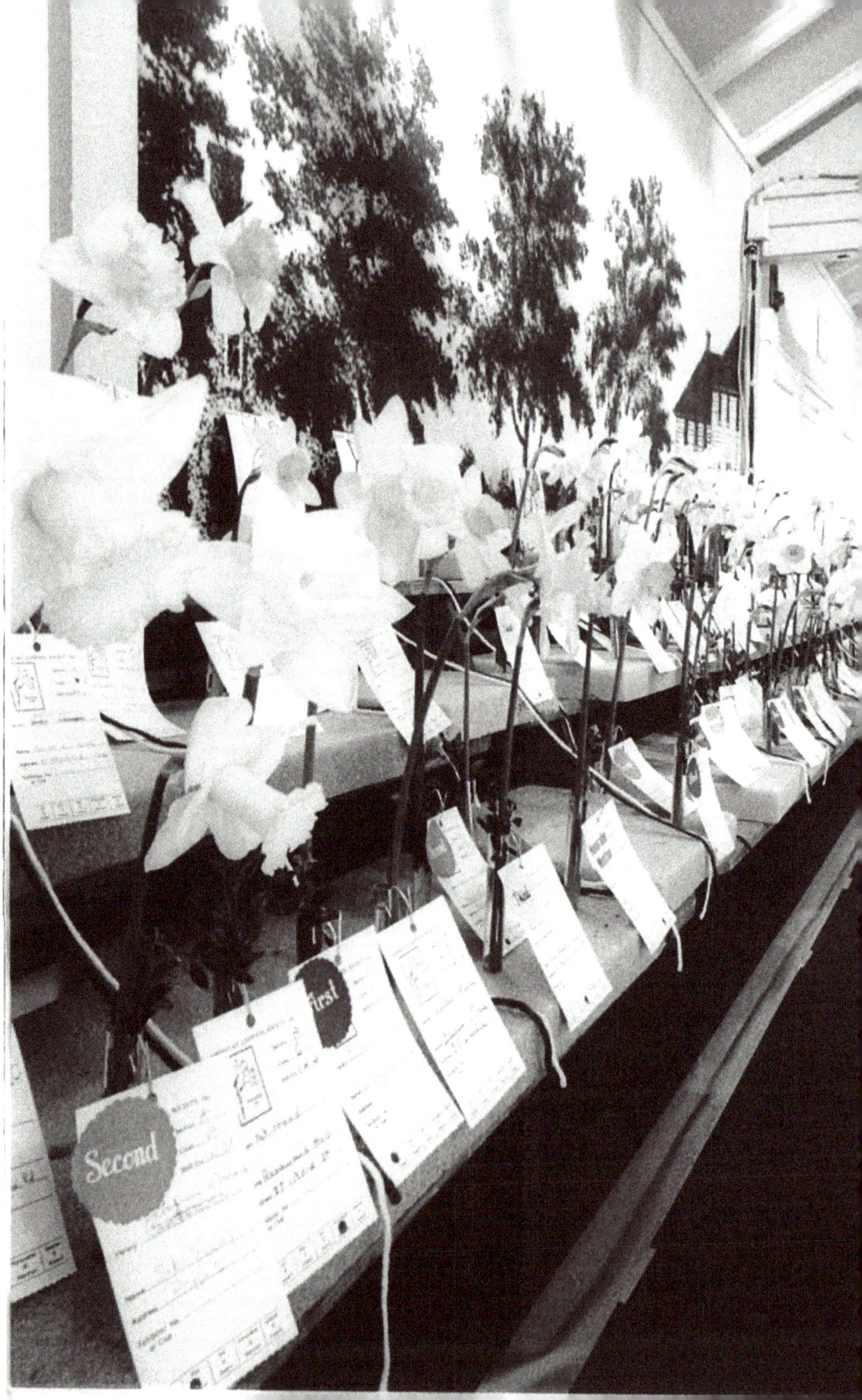

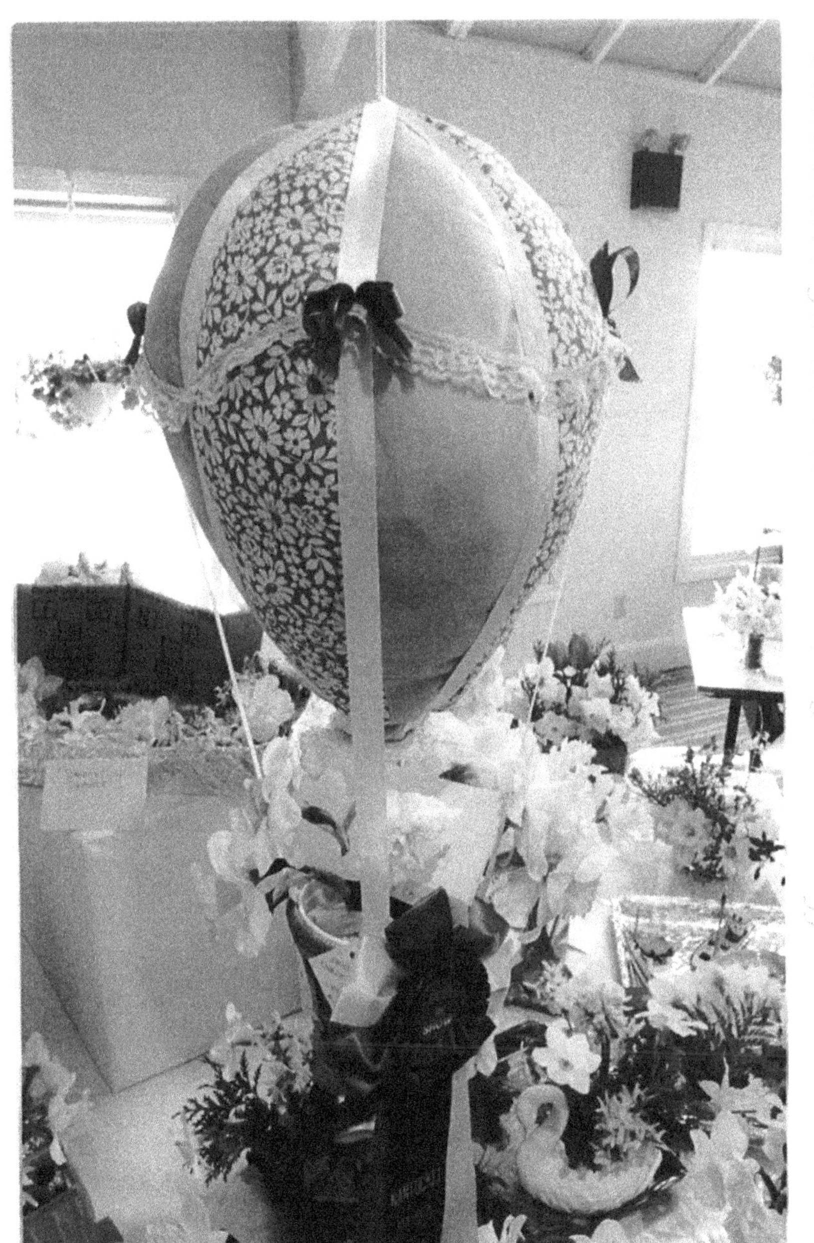

Nantucket Garden Club Annual Juried Daffodil Show

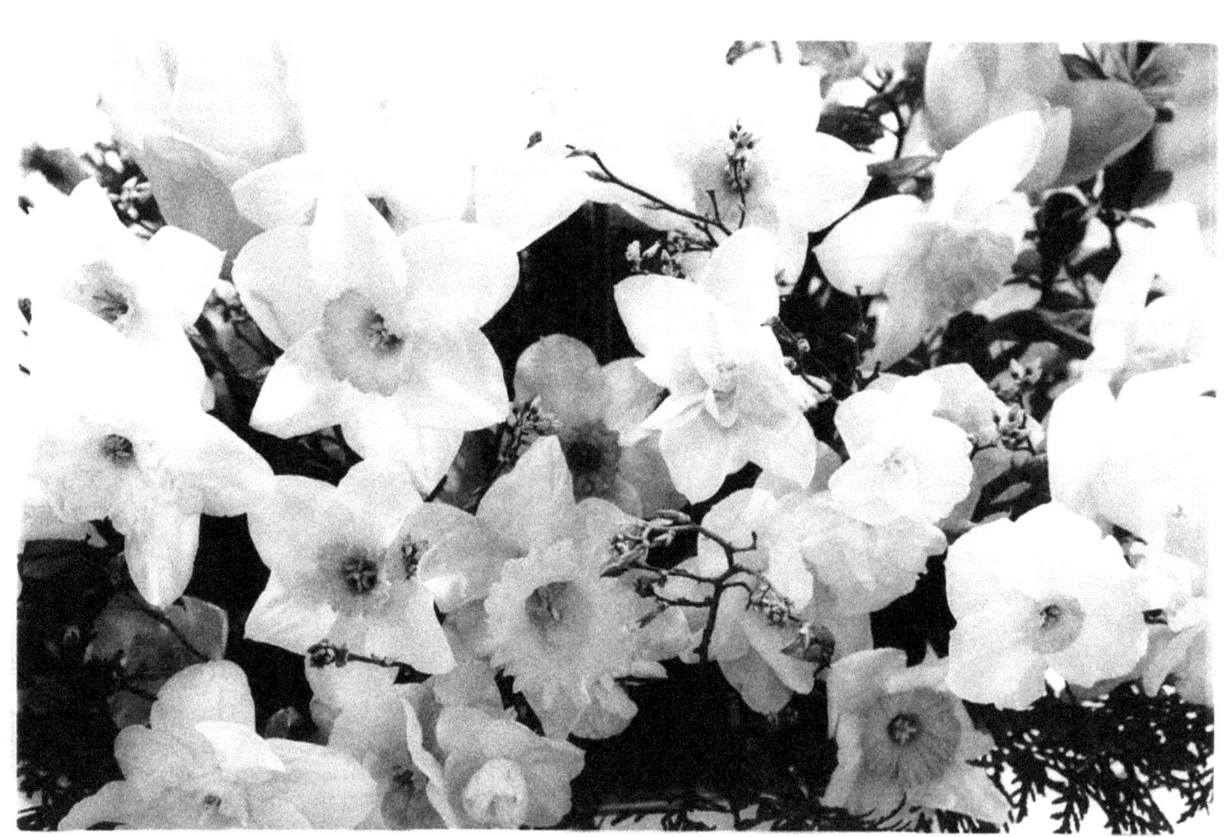

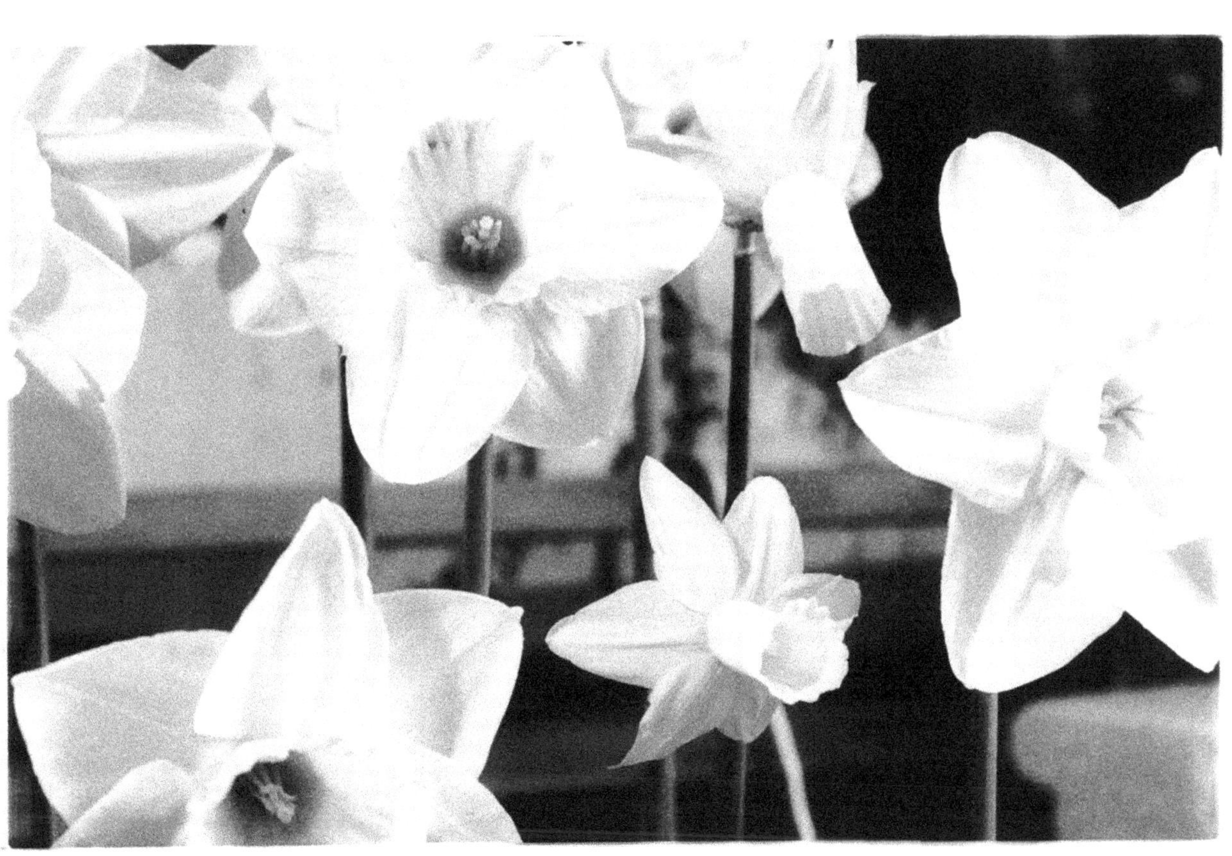

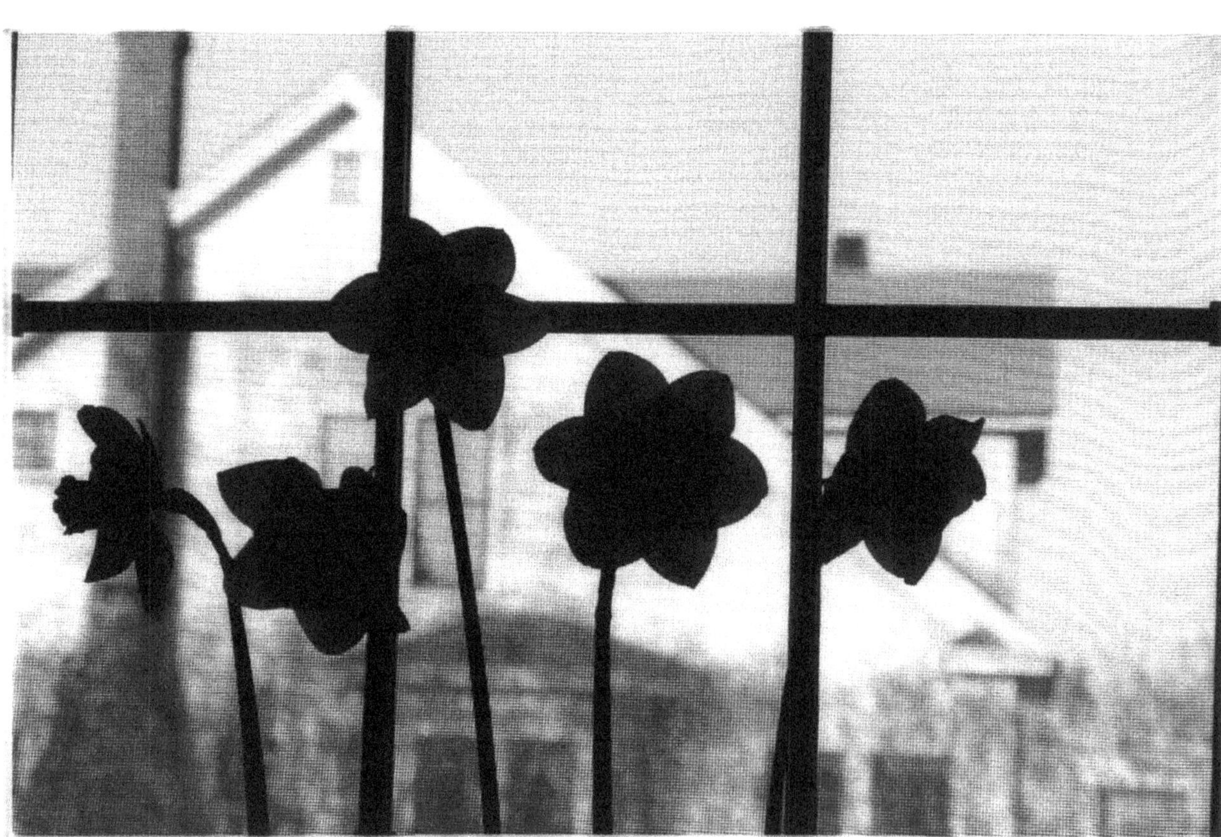

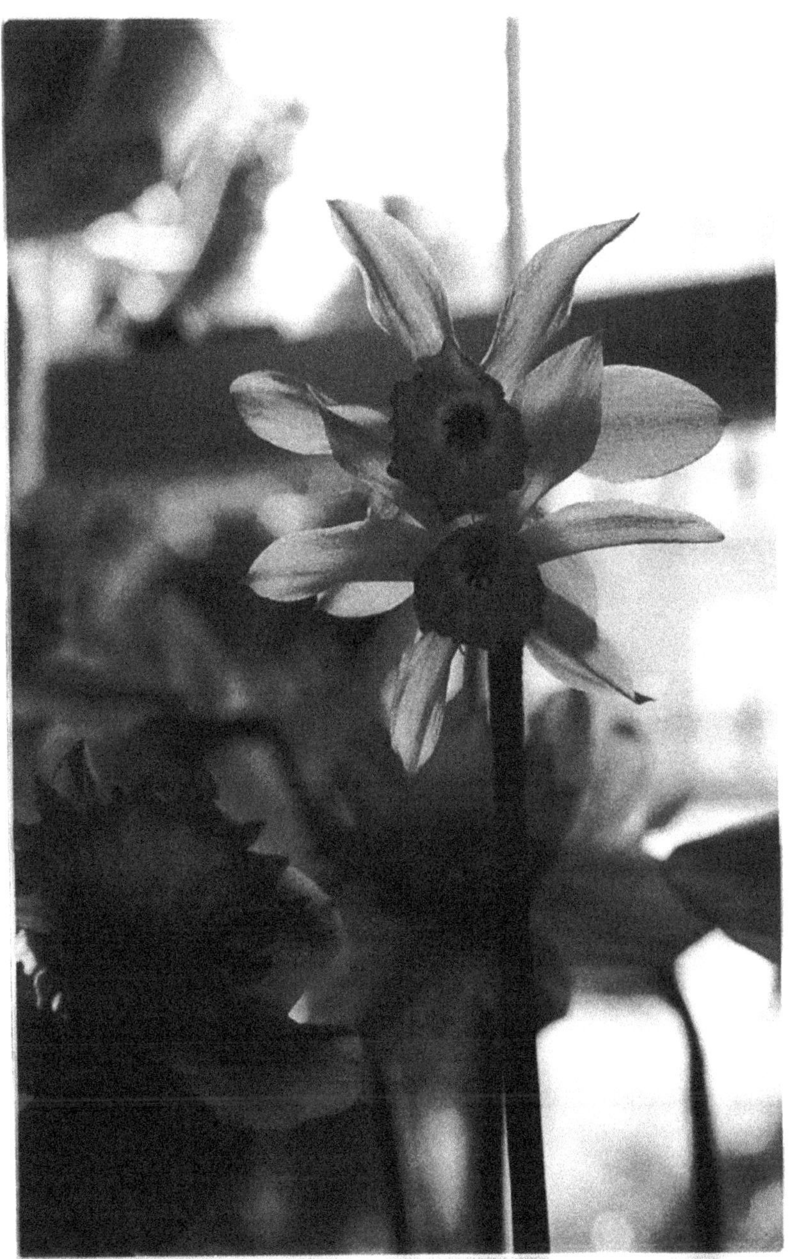

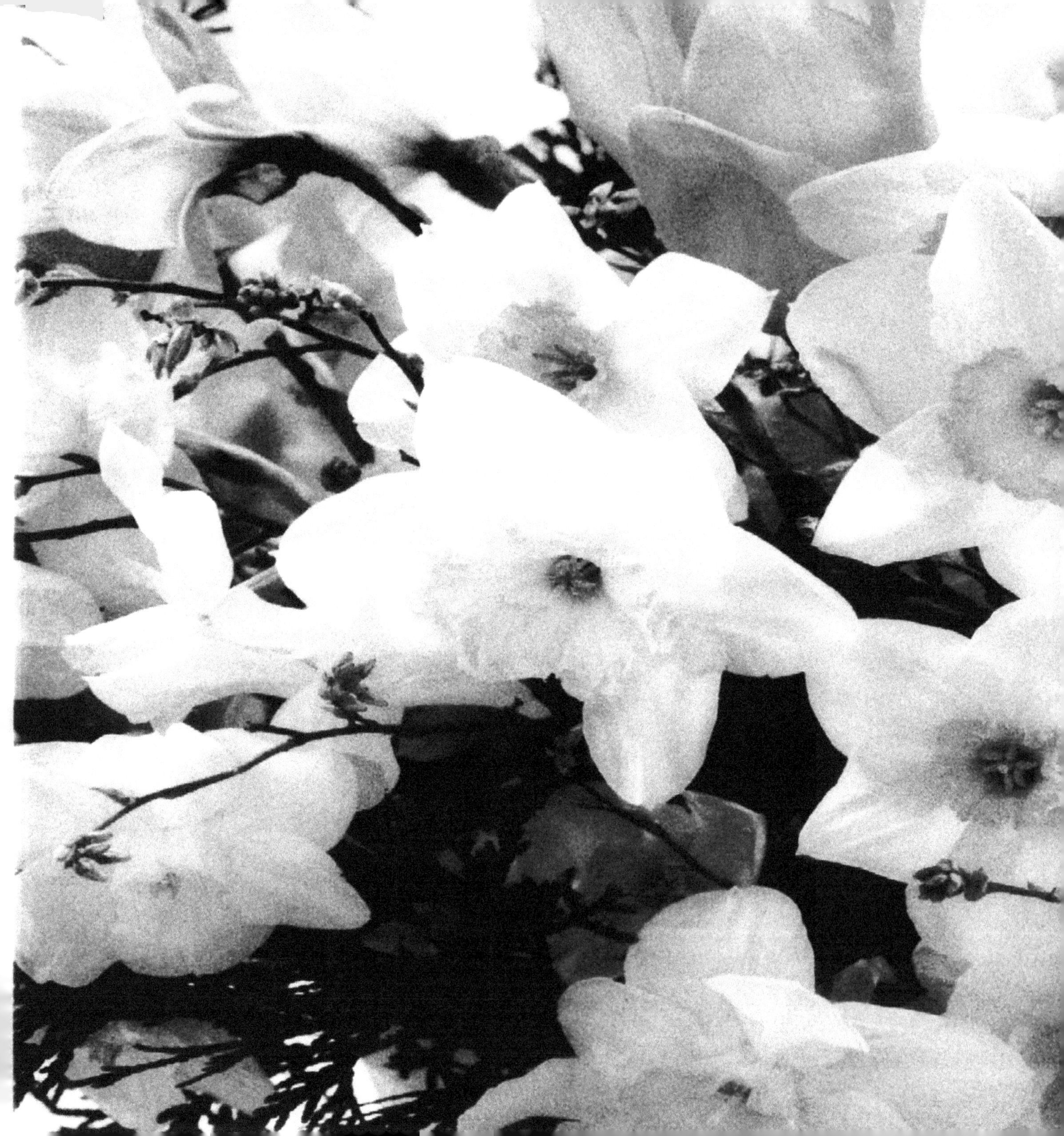

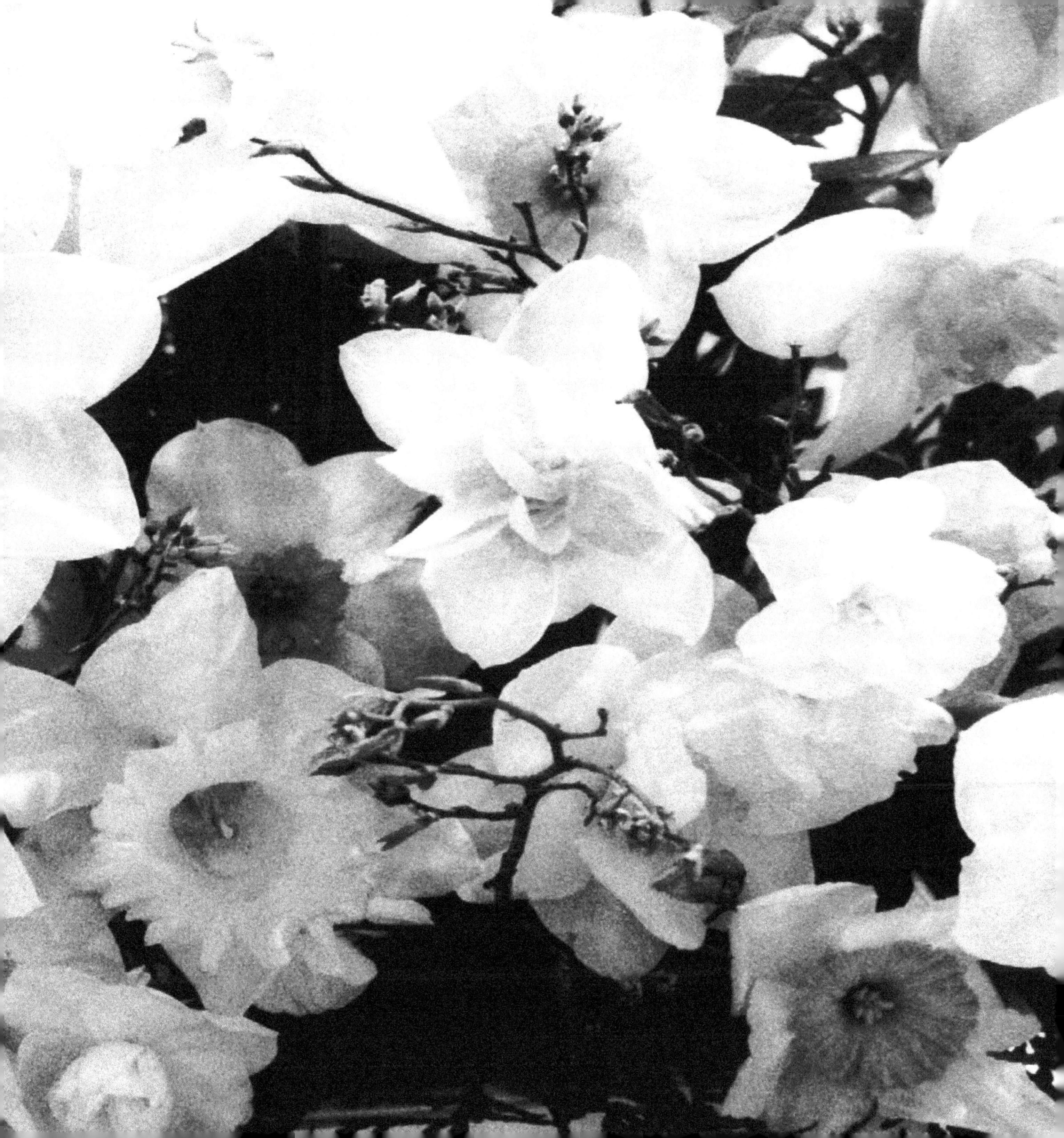

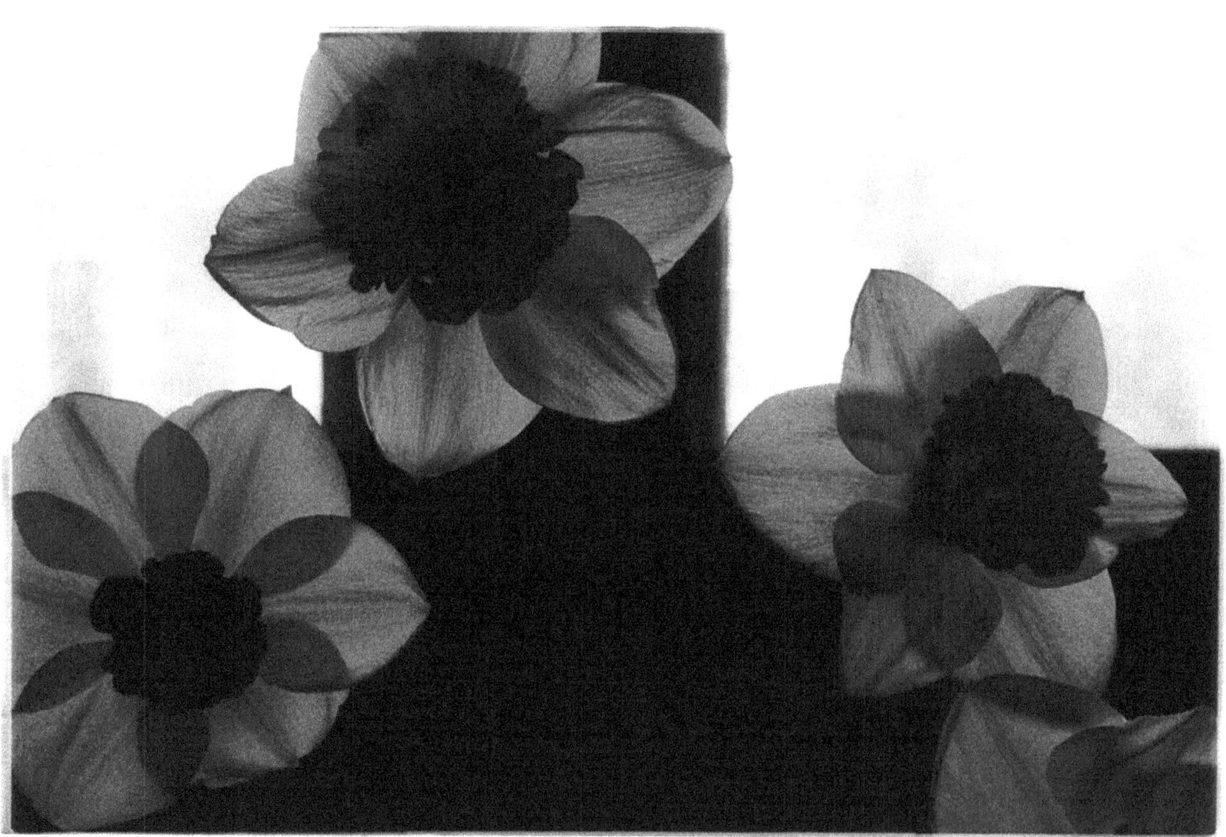

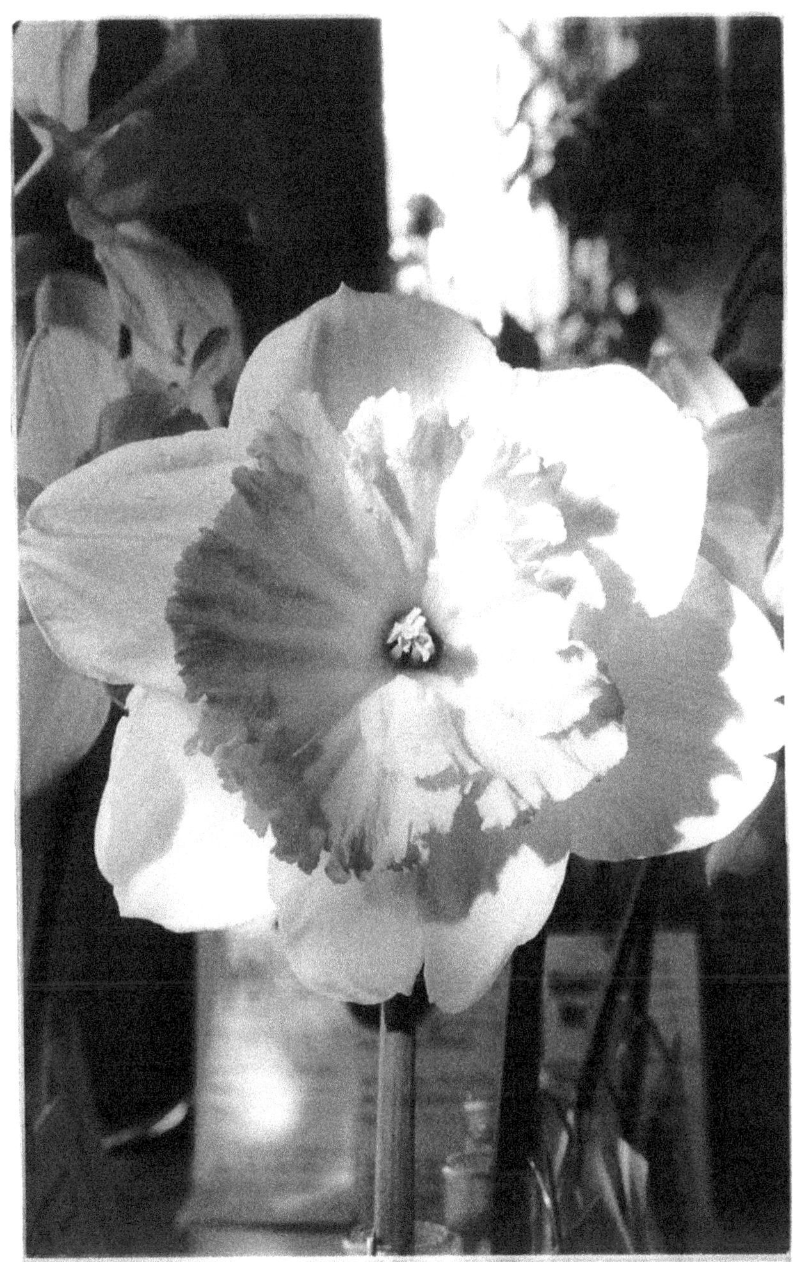

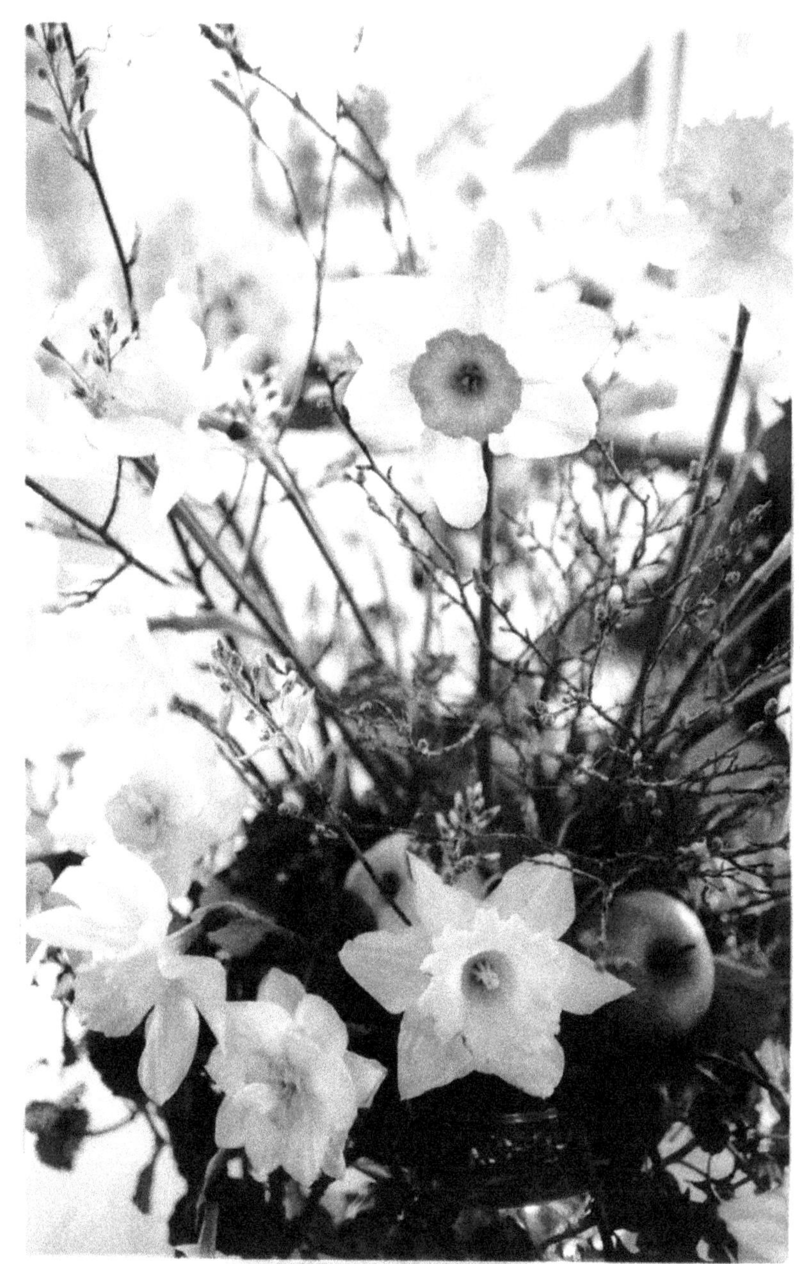

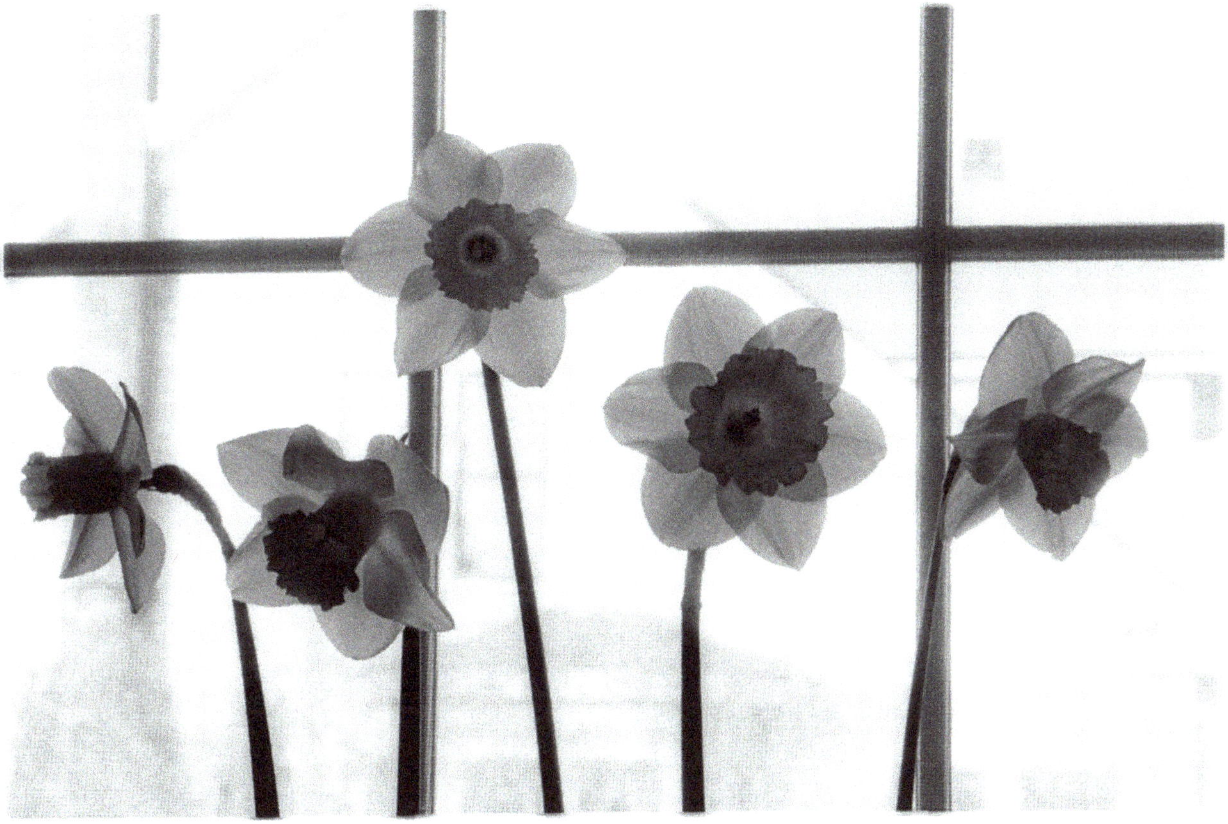

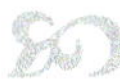

We shape our own destiny, we have dreams and ambitions, and we make choices, good ones, and bad ones. We cannot change the past, but it's never too late to change the future.

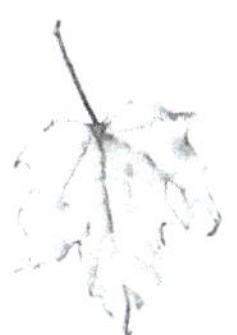

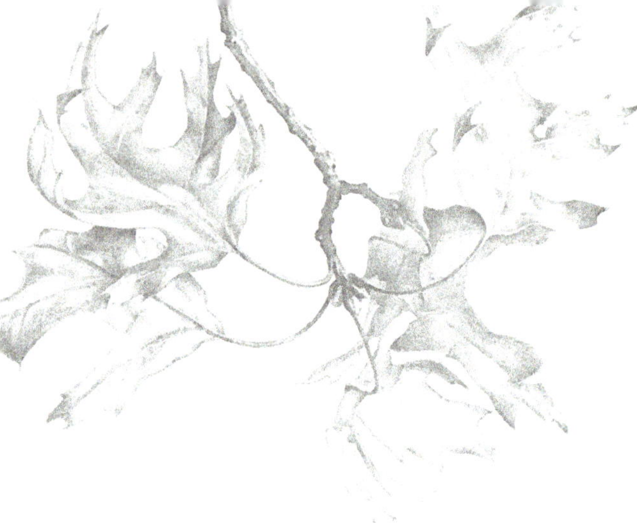

Other Books by Jack Blade

Book One - *Nantucket Island Images* - A Photographic Essay
Book Three - *Nantucket Christmas Stroll* - A Photographic Essay

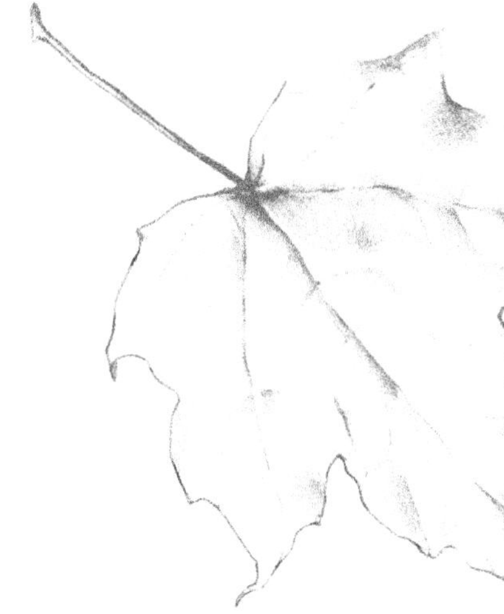

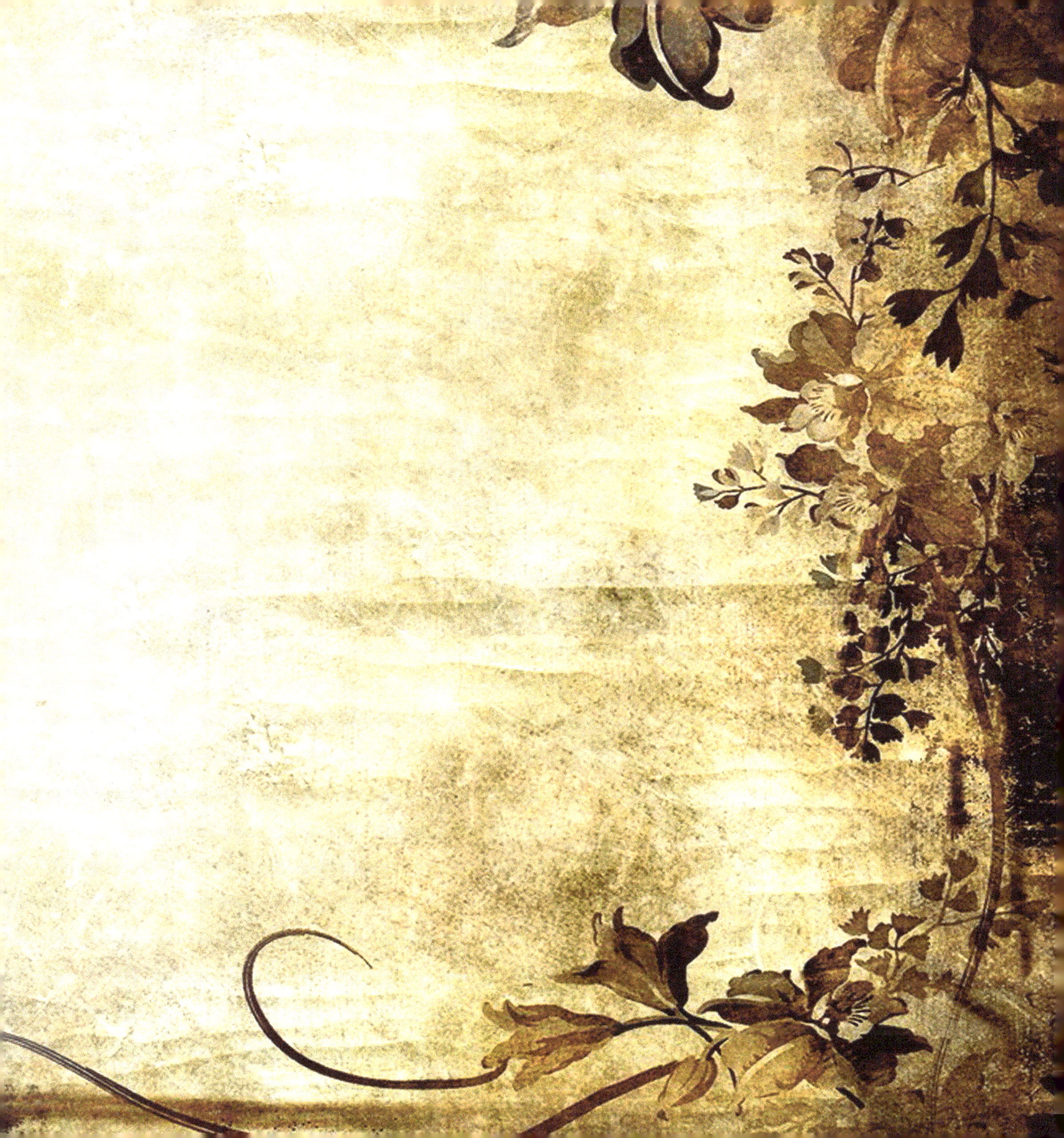

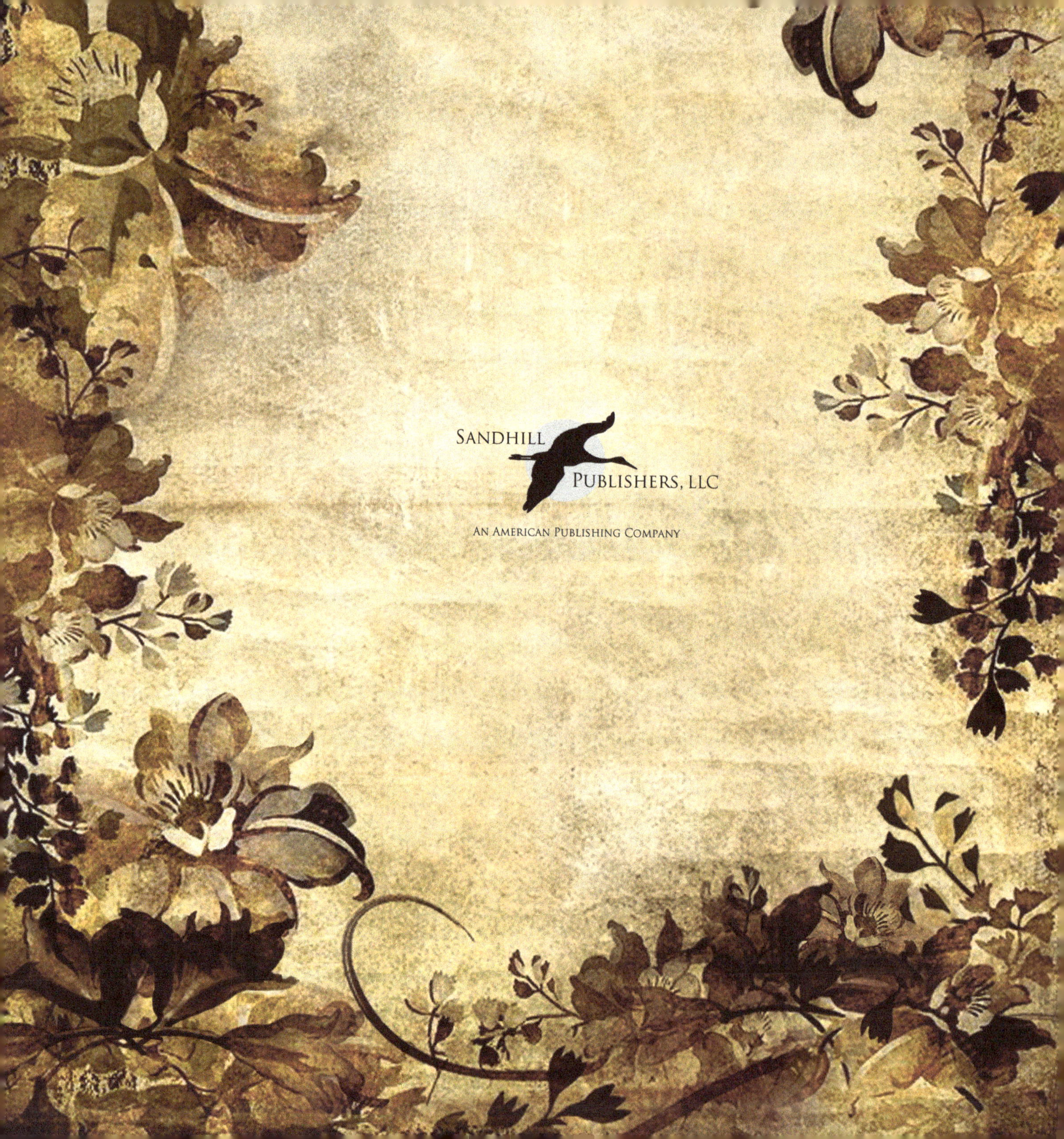

SANDHILL
PUBLISHERS, LLC
AN AMERICAN PUBLISHING COMPANY

www.ingramcontent.com/pod-product-compliance
Ingram Content Group UK Ltd.
Pitfield, Milton Keynes, MK11 3LW, UK
UKHW062003290726
14090UKWH00022B/1365

9 780998 471631